God's Parenting Game

A Quick Start and Troubleshooting Guide for Raising Christians

By Todd and Amanda Murfitt

Copyright © 2025 Todd and Amanda Murfitt
All rights reserved.

No part of this publication may be reproduced, distributed, or transmitted in any form or by any means, including photocopying, recording, or other electronic or mechanical methods, without the prior written permission of the author, except in the case of brief quotations used in reviews and certain other non-commercial uses permitted by copyright law.

This book is intended to provide general parenting tips and advice for informational purposes only. The author is not responsible for any questionable parenting hacks you attempt at 3 a.m. while sleep-deprived. Always consult with a trusted professional for specific medical, emotional, or developmental concerns.

God's Parenting Game: Quick Start and Troubleshooting Guide for Raising Christians is a work of original content. Any resemblance to actual games, cheat codes, or villains is purely coincidental (though we're looking at you, Sleep Deprivation Demon).

First Edition: 2025
Published by Murfitt Elevation

ISBN 978-1-7638370-3-4

For inquiries, visit murfittelevation.com.au

For every parent brave enough to enter God's Parenting Game without a pause button or cheat codes.

And to the tiny humans who teach us that leveling up isn't about getting it right—it's about showing up.

Table of Contents

Welcome to God's Parenting Game — 1
Introduction: Press Start to Begin

Level 1: The Baby Stage (0–12 Months) — 3
Big Boss: The Sleep Deprivation Demon
Save Point: Cuddles That Recharge

Level 2: The Toddler Stage (1–3 Years) — 18
Big Boss: The Snack Bandit
Save Point: Belly Laughs During Bathtime

Level 3: The Threenager Years (3–5 Years) — 35
Big Boss: The Tantrum Tornado
Save Point: The Magic of Storytime

Level 4: The School Years (6–9 Years) — 52
Big Boss: The Homework Hydra
Save Point: Family Dinners That Actually Happen

Level 5: The Tween Years (10–12 Years) — 69
Big Boss: The Peer Pressure Phantom
Save Point: Traditions and Check-ins

Level 6: The Teen Years (13–18 Years) — 84
Big Boss: The Eye Roll Master
Cheat Codes: Active Listening and Selective Memory
Save Point: Car Rides with Unexpected Honesty

Final Boss Battle — 101
Surviving Parenthood and Keeping Your Sanity Intact

Epilogue — 114
Parenting Pro Mode: Lessons Learned and Game Over

Afterward and Resources — 115
The new '3R's'
Emergency Help (RAGE! – tear out if needed!)
Parent Power-Ups
QR Code References

Notes and Scribbles — 141

Welcome to God's Parenting Game

Congratulations! You've officially embarked on the most chaotic, hilarious, and heart-expanding adventure of your life: **parenting.** Unlike most games, there's no instruction manual (well, except for the Bible—more on that later), no pause button, and no option to rage quit. There are, however, plenty of glitches, unexpected side quests, and boss battles along the way. But don't worry—**God has equipped you for this mission.**

This book is your **Quick Start Guide** for raising the tiny humans God has entrusted to you. Whether you're holding a newborn, chasing a toddler, or negotiating with a tiny dictator over bedtime snacks, you'll find **practical wisdom, biblical encouragement, and even a few cheat codes (aka grace and prayer) to help you level up.**

"Start children off on the way they should go, and even when they are old they will not turn from it." — Proverbs 22:6

Why This Book Exists

Let's be real: parenting books can be overwhelming. Some are so heavy on philosophy they forget that **parents need actual solutions.** Others are so focused on survival tactics they miss the bigger picture—like the fact that **God designed parenting to be about connection, love, and ultimately pointing our kids back to Him.**

This book is different. It's **short enough to read during nap time** (because let's face it, sleep is a luxury), packed with **real-**

world advice, biblical wisdom, and plenty of humour— because God gave us laughter as a survival tool.

"A cheerful heart is good medicine, but a crushed spirit dries up the bones."
— Proverbs 17:22

What to Expect

This isn't a book you have to read cover to cover. Think of it as your **parenting strategy guide:**

🎮 **Facing a bedtime meltdown?** Flip to **Level 3: Threenager Chaos** for some sanity-saving strategies.

🎮 **Feeling disconnected from your kid?** Skim the **"Save Point"** sections for quick ways to reset and reconnect.

🎮 **Need a laugh?** Check out the **Big Boss Battles**—we've all faced the Sleep Deprivation Demon (but hey, so did Jesus—Mark 4:38).

You'll also find **scriptural encouragement, prayer prompts, and quick, actionable tips** you can implement immediately. Keep your **Bible app handy** (you know your phone is within reach anyway).

Above all, remember this: **God doesn't expect you to be a perfect parent.** He just asks you to show up, rely on Him, and love your kids with all your heart.

"But He said to me, 'My grace is sufficient for you, for My power is made perfect in weakness.'" — 2 Corinthians 12:9

Press Start to Begin.

Level 1

The Baby Stage (0-12 Months)

Welcome to the tutorial level, Player 1! Your baby has officially arrived—**with minimal instructions, frequent glitches, and a primary mission: keep them alive, figure out what they want, and survive on almost no sleep.**

This stage is filled with firsts: **first cuddles, first sleepless nights, and your first realisation that nappy blowouts are proof we live in a fallen world.** But most importantly, this is where you begin building a bond with your baby—**a foundation that will carry them through every level to come.**

Pro tip: God doesn't expect perfection—He calls you to **be present.** Every time you show up for your baby—even when you're exhausted, clueless, or covered in spit-up—you're teaching them that they are loved, safe, and can trust you. And that, my friend, is **the ultimate cheat code** for parenting.

"Whoever welcomes one of these little children in My name welcomes Me." — Mark 9:37

Core Mission: Build the Bond

At this stage, your baby has one primary concern: **"Is someone here for me?"** Their tiny heart is wired to seek connection and security, and your role is to **show them love in a way that reflects God's love for us.** When you respond to their cries, hold them close, and meet their needs, you're doing more than just keeping them alive—**you're laying a foundation of trust that shapes their understanding of relationships, love, and ultimately, faith.**

But here's the good news: **Connection doesn't require expensive baby gadgets, Pinterest-perfect parenting, or a degree in infant psychology.** The best bonding moments happen in the simplest ways:

🍼 **When you lock eyes during a midnight feeding, your gaze reminds them they are seen—just as God sees us.** (*Genesis 16:13*)

🎶 **When you hum a tune while rocking them to sleep, your voice becomes their comfort—just as God quiets us with His love.** (*Zephaniah 3:17*)

🤱 **When you comfort their cries, even while running on fumes, you model the steadfast love God has for His children.** (*Psalm 34:18*)

These moments may feel small, **but they are sacred.** Every cuddle, every goofy face, every whispered **"We've got this"** is a reflection of the unconditional love God designed for families.

"We love because He first loved us." — 1 John 4:19

So embrace this stage—even the sleep-deprived chaos—knowing that your love is shaping your child's heart, one cuddle at a time.

Level 1: Accepted.

Big Boss Battle: The Sleep Deprivation Demon

This villain is relentless. **It lurks in the shadows, waiting for the moment you think you've got things under control.** It thrives on exhaustion, warping your judgment, draining your energy, and whispering lies like, *"You're failing."*

But here's the truth: **You were never meant to do this in your own strength.** Even Jesus, fully God and fully human, needed rest (Mark 4:38). And guess what? **So do you.**

Defeat Strategy:

🛡 **Tag Team Mode:** *Two are better than one.* If you have a co-player (spouse, friend, or fellow parent), take turns on night shifts so neither of you gets completely wiped out. **Even Moses needed help holding up his arms during battle** (*Exodus 17:12*), so don't be afraid to lean on your teammates.

😴 **Power Nap Buff:** *"Come to me, all you who are weary and burdened, and I will give you rest."* — *Matthew 11:28*
Nap when the baby naps. Yes, it's cliché, but it works. Even 15 minutes can feel like a **holy recharge.**

6

Summon Allies: Call in reinforcements. A grandparent, a neighbour, or even a **delivery driver bearing coffee** can be your MVP. **Remember, God often provides strength through community.** You don't have to do this alone (*Galatians 6:2*).

 Pro tip: Perfectionism has no place in this battle. Your only mission is survival. And in Christ, even survival is a victory.

"My grace is sufficient for you, for My power is made perfect in weakness." — 2 Corinthians 12:9

So grab that nap, **drink that coffee, and don't listen to the Sleep Deprivation Demon's lies.** You've got this. More importantly— **God's got you.**

Gameplay Hazards

Just like any game, parenting comes with unexpected obstacles. **Some are just minor bugs, while others feel like full-on boss battles.** But fear not, Player 1—**you are not alone.** God has equipped you with wisdom, patience (though it's still downloading), and the ability to call for divine backup when needed (*James 1:5*).

🛠 The Crying Glitch
Babies cry—it's their built-in alarm system. Sometimes the cause is obvious (**hunger, wet nappy, existential baby crisis**), and sometimes it's a complete mystery. But just because you don't understand their language yet doesn't mean you're failing. **Even God hears and responds when we cry out to Him** (*Psalm 34:17*), and you're doing the same for your little one.

🛠 Fix: Run the Troubleshooting Checklist
1. Is the baby hungry? (*Matthew 6:26 – God provides for every need, even the tiniest sparrow—and definitely your baby.*)
2. Are they wet or dirty? (*Because let's be honest—nobody is happy in a messy situation.*)

3. Are they tired or overstimulated? (*Even Jesus needed quiet time away from the crowds—Mark 6:31.*)
4. Try the **5 S's**: *Swaddle, Side position, Shush, Swing, Suck (a pacifier or feed)*. These tricks mimic the comfort of the womb—**and God's perfect design for babies to feel safe.**

🗣️ The Advice Avalanche

From strangers in the grocery store to your great-aunt on Facebook, **everyone has an opinion on how you should raise your baby.** Some advice will be helpful, some outdated, and some will make you want to throw a nappy at the wall.

🛠️ Fix: Think of Advice Like Side Quests

> 🎮 **You don't have to accept every one.** Some are worth exploring; others are best ignored.
>
> 🎮 **Smile, nod, and filter everything through wisdom and prayer.** (*Proverbs 3:5-6 – Trust in the Lord, not just random parenting hacks.*)
>
> 🎮 **Remember, God has given YOU this child for a reason.** Seek counsel, but ultimately trust that **He chose you to be this baby's parent on purpose.** (*Jeremiah 1:5*)

 **Pro Tip: Not every problem has a perfect fix, but every challenge is an opportunity to lean on God's grace.**

"Cast all your anxiety on Him because He cares for you." — 1 Peter 5:7
So breathe, Player 1. **You've got this.**

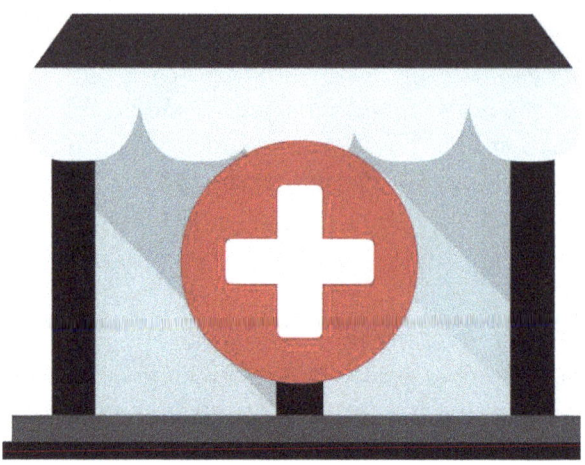

Cheat Codes for Level 1

Great news, Player 1! **Parenting may not have a pause button, but it does have a few cheat codes**—God-designed hacks to help you survive (and maybe even thrive) in the newborn stage. *"Every good and perfect gift is from above."* — James 1:17

🎵 **The White Noise Buff**
White noise machines (or apps) are **a gift straight from heaven.** They mimic the womb's comforting sounds, helping babies (and you) sleep better. **Bonus points if it drowns out barking dogs, noisy neighbors, or that Netflix binge you refuse to give up.**

📖 **Biblical Parallel:** *Even Jesus calmed the storm with His voice—so a little white noise? Totally justified.* (Mark 4:39)

👶 **One-Handed Ninja Skill**
Master the **sacred art of one-handed parenting.** Eating, brushing your teeth, making coffee—**all possible with practice (and maybe a baby carrier).**

📖 **Biblical Parallel:** *God equips us for the tasks He gives us.* So if He called you to parent, **He'll give you the skills to make it work.** (*Exodus 4:12 – "I will help you speak and will teach you what to say."*)

🙇 Cuddle Reset Button

Overwhelmed? **Hold your baby close and just breathe together.** Skin-to-skin contact isn't just comforting—it's a **God-designed reset button** for both of you.

📖 **Biblical Parallel:** *Just like we find peace in God's presence, your baby finds peace in yours.* (*Psalm 131:2 – "I have calmed and quieted my soul, like a weaned child with its mother."*)

🎮 **Pro Tip: These little moments of grace aren't just survival tools—they're sacred. You were made for this mission, and God is with you in every level.**

"The Lord will fight for you; you need only to be still." — Exodus 14:14
Now, go forth and ninja-parent with confidence!

4o

Save Point: The Power of Pause

Amid the chaos of Level 1, there will be moments that **take your breath away.** Your baby's tiny fingers wrapped around yours, holding on like you're their whole world. The way they completely melt against your chest when they fall asleep, their soft breaths syncing with yours—**creating a moment of calm in the middle of the storm.**

These moments are your **Save Point**—a **divine pause,** a chance to **breathe, recharge, and remember that this exhausting stage is also sacred.** They remind you that, despite the mess, the sleepless nights, and the overwhelming doubts, **you are building something extraordinary.**

📖 **Biblical Parallel:** Even Jesus took time to pause, to be still, and to find rest in the Father (*Mark 6:31*). If the Son of God needed quiet moments, **so do you.**

In these fleeting seconds, **time stands still.** You're not just surviving—you're **connecting.** You are shaping a tiny human who trusts you completely. And in a deeper way, **you are** experiencing a glimpse of the Father's love for us—how He holds us, comforts us, and never lets us go *(Isaiah 49:16)*.

 Pro Tip: Don't rush past these moments. They're fleeting, but they will **fuel you for every boss battle ahead.**

"Be still, and know that I am God." — Psalm 46:10

So breathe, Player 1. **This moment is holy.**

Side Quests

Not every parenting moment is a **main mission**—some are **side quests** that make the journey richer. These small but powerful moments **build connection, encourage growth, and create memories** that will last long beyond Level 1.

📖 **Biblical Bonus:** *Jesus often used small, simple acts—like breaking bread or speaking a kind word—to create deep and lasting impact. The little things matter. (Luke 24:30-31)*

🗺️ TUMMY TIME TREASURE HUNT

◆ **Objective:** Help your baby **build strength** during tummy time.

◆ **How to Play:** Lay your baby on a soft surface and place **colourful toys, a mirror, or even an open Bible** within reach. Cheer them on as they lift their head or wiggle toward the treasures.

◆ **Reward:** A stronger baby and **joyful moments** as you celebrate their progress.

📖 **Biblical Parallel:** *Encouragement makes all the difference. Just as God cheers us on in our race (Hebrews 12:1), your baby thrives when you cheer for them.*

🎵 LULLABY REMIX QUEST

◆ **Objective:** Create a **personalised lullaby** for your baby.

◆ **How to Play:** Use their name, funny rhymes, or even **scripture-based lyrics** in a simple tune. Sing it during bedtime or fussy moments.

◆ **Reward:** A **calming bedtime ritual** that becomes a **special bonding moment**—and maybe even a song they'll remember for life.

📖 **Biblical Parallel:** *God rejoices over us with singing—so it makes sense that your voice is a comfort to your child!* (*Zephaniah 3:17*)

Troubleshooting Guide

Issue	Fix
My baby only sleeps during the day, not at night.	Help them distinguish day from night by keeping daytime bright and active, and nighttime dark and quiet.
They're crying, but I've checked everything.	Sometimes babies cry to release tension. Hold them close and offer comfort—it's okay if they don't stop immediately.
I'm overwhelmed by advice from everyone.	Politely thank people for their input, then trust your instincts. Not every piece of advice is meant for you or your baby.
They won't latch during breastfeeding.	Consult a lactation consultant or try different positions. Remember, fed is best—whether it's breast milk, formula, or a combination.
They scream during nappy changes.	Distract them with a small toy or sing a silly song. A warm wipe can also help if they're startled by the cold.
I feel like I'm failing as a parent.	You're not. Parenting is hard, and perfection isn't the goal. Celebrate small wins and remind yourself that showing up is what matters most.
I never get time for myself.	Build short self-care moments into your day—a 10-minute shower, a cup of tea, or guilt-free scrolling while the baby naps.
My baby hates tummy time.	Start small, even 30 seconds, and make it fun with toys or your face at their level. Try tummy time on your chest if the floor is too overwhelming.

Pro Tip for Cheat Codes and Troubleshooting

Every baby is different. **What works one day might not work the next—and that's okay.** Parenting isn't about having all the answers; **it's about showing up, staying flexible, and trusting that God is guiding you as you learn the game.**

"Trust in the Lord with all your heart and lean not on your own understanding." — Proverbs 3:5
You've got this. More importantly, **God's got you.**

Level 2

The Toddler Stage (1-3 Years)

Congratulations! You've Leveled Up to The Toddler Stage.

Welcome to **Level 2: Toddler Mode**, where your once-cuddly baby has evolved into a **highly mobile, snack-demanding mini-boss with a flair for drama.** This stage is the **open-world portion of the game**—your toddler has **free roam, zero impulse control, and a personal mission to test every boundary known to humanity.**

Your primary missions? **Survive tantrums, manage chaos, and encourage independence**—all while keeping a straight face when they insist that their stuffed giraffe needs its own plate at dinner.

 Pro Tip: Toddlers don't come with a pause button, but they do come with an infinite capacity for wonder. Lean into the chaos, laugh often, and always keep snacks on hand—**Jesus Himself knew the value of a well-timed meal.** (*John 6:11*).

Core Mission: Foster Independence

Toddlers are **born explorers**, which is a polite way of saying **they will attempt to dismantle your home while making direct eye contact with you.** They're also determined to prove they **don't need you—except when they absolutely do (which is every 4.2 minutes).**

Your job? **Help them feel safe while they figure out how to be their own little person.** Just as **God gives us free will but guides us with love,** you are giving your toddler space to grow—while keeping the sharp objects out of reach.

📖 **Biblical Parallel:** *Just as God lets us explore and learn, knowing we will stumble, He is always there when we need Him. You are modeling that same steadfast love to your child. (Deuteronomy 31:8)*

How to Foster Independence

🛠 **Offer Choices**

🔹 **Toddlers crave control.** Give them small, manageable choices to **help them feel empowered without total anarchy:**

👉 "Do you want the red cup or the blue cup?"

👉 "Would you like to put on your shoes first or your jacket?"

📖 **Biblical Wisdom:** *Even God gives us choices, leading us toward wisdom while allowing us to grow. (Joshua 24:15 – "Choose for yourselves this day whom you will serve.")*

🛠 Encourage Self-Help
◆ **Celebrate every attempt** at self-sufficiency—**even if their pants are on backward and their shoes are mismatched.** It's not about perfection; it's about **effort.**

📖 **Biblical Wisdom:** *God delights in our progress, even when we're still figuring things out. (Philippians 1:6 – "He who began a good work in you will carry it on to completion.")*

🛠 Let Them Lead (Within Reason)
◆ A **10-minute walk might take 30 minutes** because they are examining every rock, leaf, and oddly shaped piece of lint on the sidewalk. That's okay—they're learning.

📖 **Biblical Wisdom:** *God never rushes our growth. Instead, He walks with us at our pace, guiding us as we explore life. (Psalm 119:105 – "Your word is a lamp to my feet and a light to my path.")*

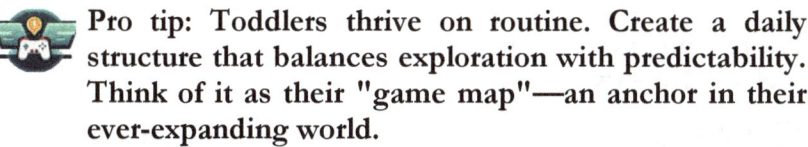 Pro tip: Toddlers thrive on routine. Create a daily structure that balances exploration with predictability. Think of it as their "game map"—an anchor in their ever-expanding world.

"For God is not a God of disorder but of peace." — *1 Corinthians 14:33*

So take a deep breath, **Player 1.** This level may be unpredictable, **but you are exactly the parent your child needs.** And most importantly—**God is with you every step of the way.** 🎮✨

Listen

Big Boss Battle: The Snack Bandit

This villain lurks in your kitchen, **demanding crackers, cookies, or—without fail—the one snack you don't have in stock.** The **Snack Bandit** strikes at the worst times: **right before meals, in the middle of grocery store trips, and during car rides when your emergency stash is just out of reach.**

But fear not, Player 1! **You have the tools to defeat this carb-fueled adversary.**

📖 **Biblical Parallel:** Just like **we don't live by bread alone but by every word from God** (*Matthew 4:4*), toddlers don't actually need snacks every second of the day—they just *think* they do.

Defeat Strategy

🛡 **Preload Inventory**

🔹 Keep a **snack arsenal** in every **bag, pocket, and glove compartment.** Think **easy-to-grab, low-mess options** like fruit pouches, pretzels, or **biblically inspired** (aka not-too-sticky) dried fruit.

📖 **Biblical Wisdom:** *Joseph stored up grain for future famine—so you, too, must prepare for toddler snack emergencies.* (*Genesis 41:48*)

22

🛡️ Limit Power-Ups

🔹 Snacks are fine, but don't let them **replace actual meals.** Set **snack windows** and stick to them. If a meltdown is looming, remind them, **"The feast is coming soon!"**

📖 **Biblical Wisdom:** *God provides for our needs at the right time—not always the moment we demand it. (Philippians 4:19 – "My God will supply all your needs according to His riches in glory.")*

🛡️ Diversion Tactics

🔹 When the **Snack Bandit** strikes **outside of snack time,** use creative redirection:

👉 **"How about a dance party instead?"**

👉 **"Let's read a story first, then check on snack time."**

👉 **"Can you help me pick out what we'll eat for lunch?"**

📖 **Biblical Wisdom:** **Jesus often redirected people from what they thought they needed to what actually nourished them. (John 6:35 – "I am the bread of life.")*

🎮 **Pro tip: Toddlers don't snack because they're hungry. They snack because they're bored. Be one step ahead— just like God is always one step ahead of us.**

"Before a word is on my tongue, You, Lord, know it completely." — Psalm 139:4

You've got this, Player 1. **Now go forth and outwit the Snack Bandit!** 🥕🎮

Gameplay Hazards

Every game has its unexpected glitches, and Level 2: Toddler Mode is packed with bugs, boss fights, and challenges that require patience, strategy, and sometimes a deep breath (or five). The good news? God equips you for every level. (*2 Timothy 3:17*)

🚨 The "No!" Monster

Your toddler has discovered their favorite word, and it's "No." They'll use it for everything—from getting dressed to eating dinner to simply existing in the same room as you.

🛠 Fix:

🎮 Turn "No" into a game: "I bet you can't say 'Yes'?" (Toddlers love proving you wrong.)

🎮 **Offer choices instead of commands**: "Do you want to wear the red shirt or the blue shirt?" This gives them a sense of control while keeping the chaos contained.

📖 **Biblical Parallel:** *Even in our own stubbornness, God guides us with patience and wisdom. He doesn't force obedience—He invites us to choose wisely. (Deuteronomy 30:19 – "I have set before you life and death, blessings and curses. Now choose life.")*

🚨 The Sudden Meltdown Bug

Meltdowns happen—often with no warning, and usually over something like the "wrong color socks." One minute, they're fine. The next? Tears, flailing, and the kind of dramatic sorrow Shakespeare would admire.

🛠️ Fix:

🎮 **Stay calm.** (Easier said than done, but toddlers mirror your reactions.)

🎮 **Validate their feelings:** "I see you're upset because the blue socks are in the wash. That's hard." Acknowledging their frustration helps them feel understood.

🎮 **Distract or redirect:** "Want to pick out a book while I grab your socks?"

📖 **Biblical Parallel:** *Even when we struggle,* **God doesn't dismiss our emotions—He meets us with comfort and guidance.** (*Psalm 34:18* – *"The Lord is close to the brokenhearted."*)

🚨 The Childcare Conundrum

Choosing childcare can feel overwhelming. No matter what you decide—daycare, a nanny, a family member—guilt creeps in.

🛠️ Fix:

🎮 Remember: **Childcare isn't about replacing you.** It's about finding the right support system for your family.

🎮 Visit options, pray for wisdom, and trust your gut. God has entrusted you with this child, and He will guide your decisions. (*James 1:5*)

🎮 **Your love and connection at home are what truly shape your child.** Quality matters more than quantity.

📖 **Reassurance:** *Choosing childcare doesn't make you a bad parent—it makes you a resourceful one.* Even Moses' mother had to trust someone else with her child for a time—and God still had a plan for him. (*Exodus 2:3-10*)

Pro tip: Not every problem has an instant fix**, but God's grace covers every struggle.** You're not just raising a child—you're shaping a future disciple, and God walks with you in every challenge.

"The Lord gives strength to His people; the Lord blesses His people with peace." — Psalm 29:11

Take heart, Player 1. You're doing better than you think. 🚀✨

watch

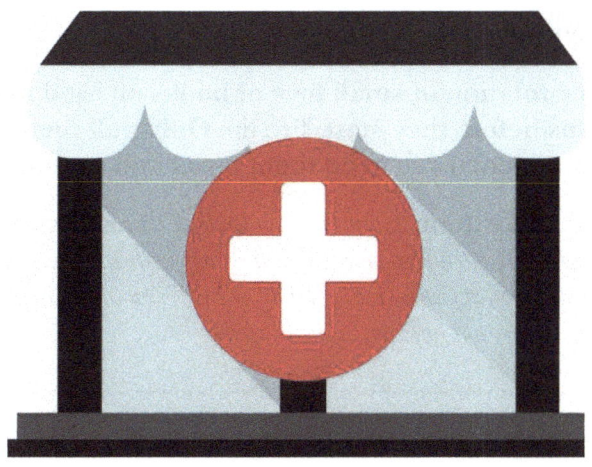

Cheat Codes for Level 2

Welcome to **Level 2**, where toddlers are powered by **pure determination, boundless energy, and an uncanny ability to say "No" before breakfast.** But don't worry—**you've got cheat codes.**

📖 **Biblical Bonus:** *Even God gives us tools to make parenting easier. Whether it's wisdom, patience, or the occasional well-placed distraction, He's got you covered. (James 1:5)*

🏆 **Sticker Chart Magic**

🔹 **Motivation is everything.** Toddlers love **instant rewards**, so a **sticker chart** for tasks like **brushing teeth, tidying toys, or staying in bed past 5 AM** can work wonders.

📖 **Biblical Parallel:** *God encourages us with rewards, too! He knows that sometimes, a little motivation helps us stay on track. (Colossians 3:23-24 – "Whatever you do, work at it with all your heart... since you know that you will receive an inheritance from the Lord as a reward.")*

🔄 Pre-emptive Distraction

🔹 **Keep a rotation of small toys or books** on hand to **prevent meltdowns before they start.** Pro tip: **Only pull them out during emergencies** to **keep them novel and exciting.**

📖 **Biblical Wisdom:** *Even Jesus understood that redirection is a powerful tool—He often responded to distractions with wisdom, guiding people toward a better focus. (Luke 10:41-42 – "You are worried and upset about many things, but only one thing is needed.")*

📱 Screen Time: The Double-Edged Sword

🔹 **Screen time can save your sanity**, but use it wisely.

🎮 **Choose educational shows** (*hello, Bluey!*) instead of mindless entertainment.

🎮 **Set clear limits** to avoid the **Screen Time Monster**—aka **toddler rage when you turn it off.**

🎮 **Use it as a tool, not a babysitter.**

📖 **Biblical Balance:** *There's a time for everything—including rest. Technology can be helpful, but balance is key. (Ecclesiastes 3:1 – "To everything there is a season, and a time for every purpose under heaven.")*

 Pro Tip: Toddlers thrive on **routine, encouragement, and a little creative problem-solving. You are their greatest guide in this game of life.**

"Teach them to your children, talking about them when you sit at home and when you walk along the road, when you lie down and when you get up." — Deuteronomy 11:19

Now go forth, **Player 1. Use your cheat codes wisely, and may your sticker supply never run dry!** 🚀✨

Save Point: The Belly Laugh Reset

Few things are as healing as a toddler's **deep, uncontrollable belly laugh.** That pure, joy-filled sound **bursts forth when you blow raspberries on their tummy, chase them around the house, or make goofy faces during bath time.** It's the kind of laughter that **melts away stress and exhaustion in an instant.**

These moments are your **Save Point**—a chance to **pause, breathe, and soak in the delight of toddlerhood.** They remind you that despite the tantrums, the messes, and the sheer unpredictability of this level, **it is also overflowing with joy.**

📖 **Biblical Parallel:** *Joy is a gift from God—it sustains us, lifts our spirits, and reminds us of His goodness. (Nehemiah 8:10 – "The joy of the Lord is your strength.")*

Why Laughter Matters

💛 **Laughter is a shortcut to connection.** When you share a giggle with your toddler, **you're building trust, strengthening your bond, and showing them that life—even the frustrating parts—can be filled with joy.**

♡ **Laughter resets your perspective.** No, the laundry isn't done. Yes, there are crumbs everywhere. **But in that moment of belly laughter, none of that matters.**

♡ **Laughter is a form of worship.** God created joy. **Every giggle, every squeal of delight, every goofy moment is a tiny echo of heaven.**

📖 **Biblical Parallel:** *Jesus welcomed children into His presence and delighted in them. He knew that childlike joy is a glimpse of the Kingdom of God. (Matthew 19:14)*

 Pro Tip: Don't underestimate the power of your own laughter. Let loose, **be silly, and enjoy the game.** Laughing with your toddler isn't just a survival strategy—it's a **sacred connection.**

"A cheerful heart is good medicine, but a crushed spirit dries up the bones." — *Proverbs 17:22*

So, **Player 1,** lean into the joy. **Let your toddler's laughter reset your spirit—and may your days be filled with more giggles than meltdowns.** 🎮♡✨

Side Quests!

Not every part of parenting is a **main mission**—sometimes, the best moments come from **side quests.** These fun, faith-filled adventures **build connection, spark joy, and strengthen your little one's heart and mind.**

📖 **Biblical Bonus:** *Jesus often used everyday moments to teach, connect, and bring joy. Side quests aren't distractions—they're opportunities for growth and love. (Mark 10:16)*

🏴‍☠️ TREASURE HUNT ADVENTURE

♦ **Objective:** Create a **scavenger hunt** for your toddler using toys or snacks as "treasures."

♦ **How to Play:** Hide items around the house and give **simple clues** to help your toddler **search and discover.**

♦ **Reward:** Boosts **problem-solving skills** and **creates excitement** as they explore.

📖 **Biblical Parallel:** *God promises that when we seek, we will find.* Encouraging curiosity and exploration **reflects the heart of our faith journey.** *(Matthew 7:7 – "Seek and you will find.")*

💃 DANCE-OFF SHOWDOWN

♦ **Objective:** Have a **5-minute dance party** with your toddler.

♦ **How to Play:** Play their **favorite songs**, get **silly with your moves**, and let them **lead the choreography** (yes, even if it involves jumping in circles).

♦ **Reward: Burns off energy,** lifts the mood, and **creates joyful memories** together.

Biblical Parallel: *David danced before the Lord with all his might! God delights in joyful expressions of love and freedom. (2 Samuel 6:14)*

 **Pro Tip:** These little moments **aren't just for fun**—they **teach, bond, and build lasting memories.** In a world full of distractions, taking time for **joyful play is a gift**—for your toddler **and for you.**

"There is a time for everything... a time to weep and a time to laugh, a time to mourn and a time to dance." — *Ecclesiastes 3:1,4*

Now go forth, **Player 1—embrace the side quests, and may your dance moves be as legendary as your patience!**
🎮💛✨

Troubleshooting Guide

Issue	Fix
My toddler throws food during meals.	Keep meal portions small and introduce a "no thank you" bowl for unwanted food to redirect the behaviour.
They say "no" to everything.	Offer two choices instead of yes/no questions: "Do you want the red shirt or the blue one?" Giving them control reduces power struggles.
They have meltdowns over small things.	Stay calm and acknowledge their feelings: "I see you're upset because the tower fell. That's hard." Then offer a distraction or solution.
They refuse to share with others.	Focus on turn-taking rather than sharing. "You can play with the truck for two minutes, then it's your friend's turn."
Bedtime is a battle every night.	Establish a consistent bedtime routine: bath, story, and lights out. Keep it calm and predictable to reduce resistance.
They won't sit still for anything.	Channel their energy into short, active tasks like fetching a toy or jumping on a pillow before transitioning to quieter activities.
They want to do everything themselves.	Let them try! Offer safe opportunities for independence, even if it's messy. "You can pour your cereal, and I'll help with the milk."
They bite or hit when frustrated.	Stay calm, remove them from the situation, and explain: "We don't bite. Let's use words to tell me how you're feeling."

Pro Tip for Cheat Codes and Troubleshooting

Toddlers thrive on structure and positive reinforcement. When things feel chaotic, focus on **connection and consistency—they're learning, not defying.**

📖 **Biblical Wisdom:** *"Start children off on the way they should go, and even when they are old they will not turn from it."* — Proverbs 22:6

You've got this, Player 1! Now go forth and troubleshoot like the parenting pro God made you to be. 🚀✨

Level 3

The Threenager Years (3-5 Years)

Congratulations, Player 1! You've Unlocked The Threenager Years 🎮🔥

Welcome to **Level 3: The Threenager Years**, where your toddler's **sass levels are maxed out, their emotions have no speed limit, and their negotiation skills could win them a seat at a UN summit.**

This level is all about **navigating big personalities, even bigger feelings, and the occasional full-volume meltdown in public.**

Your primary mission? **Survive the chaos while fostering their creativity, independence, and growing sense of self.**

🎖️ **Pro Tip:** Threenagers are like **mini volcanoes—unpredictable, explosive, but also capable of breathtaking beauty.** The key is to **weather the eruptions** and **treasure the quiet moments in between.**

📖 **Biblical Bonus:** *Even when life feels chaotic, God gives us peace in the storm. You are your child's steady presence, just as God is ours. (Isaiah 26:3)*

Core Mission: Embrace the Drama and Build Emotional Resilience

At this stage, your child is developing **emotional depth** and **independence,** but they **lack the tools to manage** their **big feelings.** This is where you step in—not to **fix everything** but to **guide them** in understanding and expressing their emotions.

📖 **Biblical Wisdom:** *God is slow to anger, abounding in love, and always guiding us with grace—even when we're an emotional mess. That's our model for parenting, too. (Psalm 103:8)*

How to Build Resilience

🛠 **Label Their Feelings**

◆ **Example:** "I see you're frustrated because the block tower fell. That's hard."

◆ **Why?** Naming emotions **helps them feel seen, normalizes feelings, and teaches them how to express themselves.**

📖 **Biblical Parallel:** *Even Jesus expressed emotions—anger, sadness, joy. Naming feelings isn't weakness—it's wisdom. (John 11:35 – "Jesus wept.")*

🛠 **Model Emotional Regulation**

◆ **If you stay calm during their meltdowns, you're showing them how to handle stress.** *(Easier said than done, I know!)*

◆ **Deep breaths, steady voice, and a silent prayer for patience go a long way.**

📖 **Biblical Wisdom:** *"A gentle answer turns away wrath, but a harsh word stirs up anger." — Proverbs 15:1*

🛠 **Play it Out**

◆ **Creative play is their language.**

◆ Use **puppet shows** about sharing, **toy storytelling** to talk through fears, or **role-playing** to help them process emotions.

📖 **Biblical Parallel:** *Jesus taught through parables—simple, relatable stories that helped people understand deep truths. Using play to teach emotions follows the same principle! (Matthew 13:34)*

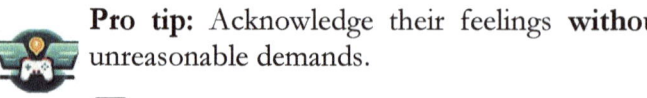 **Pro tip:** Acknowledge their feelings **without caving** to unreasonable demands.

💬 **Example:** "I know you want cookies for breakfast, but we're having oatmeal. It's okay to feel upset about that."

📖 **Biblical Encouragement:** *We don't always get what we want, but God provides what we need. (Philippians 4:19)*

Big Boss Battle: The Tantrum Tornado

Warning: The Tantrum Tornado can strike at any time. Sometimes it's because their toast was cut into **triangles instead of squares.** Other times, it's because you dared to put their shoes on the correct feet. **No one knows why.**

These emotional storms may feel **endless and personal,** but **they're not.** They are a **normal part of your child's learning curve**—their brain is **still wiring itself to handle frustration.**

📖 **Biblical Bonus:** *Even God's people had their fair share of emotional meltdowns in the wilderness, but He remained patient and loving. That's our model as parents, too! (Exodus 16:2-4)*

Defeat Strategy

🛡 **Stay Calm**

🔹 Your **calm presence helps them regulate.**

🔹 **Take deep breaths, even if they're screaming at full volume.** (Yes, even if it's happening in the grocery store.)

📖 **Biblical Parallel:** *Jesus remained calm even when storms raged around Him. Be the steady presence your child needs. (Mark 4:39 – "Peace, be still.")*

🛡️ **Set Boundaries**

🔷 Let them **feel their feelings** while holding firm to boundaries.

🔷 **Example:** "I won't let you throw toys, but I'll stay with you until you're ready to calm down."

📖 **Biblical Wisdom:** *God sets loving boundaries for us—not to restrict us, but to guide us toward what's best. (Proverbs 3:12 – "The Lord disciplines those He loves, as a father the son he delights in.")*

🛡️ **Redirect Energy**

🔷 Once the **tornado starts to fizzle, offer a distraction:**

　🎮 "Want to help me feed the dog?"
　🎮 "Can you help me find your teddy?"
　🎮 "Let's stomp our frustration out like dinosaurs!"

📖 **Biblical Example:** *When Elijah was overwhelmed, God redirected him toward rest and a renewed purpose. (1 Kings 19:11-12)*

Pro tip: 💡 **Tantrums are actually a sign of a healthy, growing brain.** Your child is **learning** to handle frustration. **Your job is to guide, not control.**

📖 **Biblical Encouragement:** *"Be completely humble and gentle; be patient, bearing with one another in love." — Ephesians 4:*

So take a deep breath, Player 1. **This battle won't last forever, but your love and patience will have a lasting impact.** 🎮✨🗿

Gameplay Hazards

With great independence comes **great challenges**, and **Level 3** is packed with **hazards that test patience, endurance, and your ability to answer 47 "Why?" questions before breakfast.**

📖 **Biblical Encouragement:** *Even in the toughest parenting moments, God gives us wisdom, strength, and (thankfully) a sense of humor. (James 1:5)*

🔄 The Question Loop

"Why? Why? Why?" Your child has entered an **infinite curiosity loop.** It's **adorable at first…** until it's the **500th question of the day.**

🛠 **Fix:**

🎮 Answer simply, then redirect:

👉 *"Why does the sun shine?"* → *"Great question! Let's draw the sun while we talk about it."*

🎮 Turn their curiosity into creativity, exploration, or a distraction.

📖 **Biblical Parallel:** *Even Jesus asked questions to spark curiosity and deeper thinking. Encourage their wonder, but don't be afraid to set limits!* (Luke 2:46-47)

🛡️ The Sharing Struggle

"MINE!" is the **battle cry of the threenager.** Sharing **does not come naturally—because at this age, everything is treasure.**

🛠️ **Fix:**

🎮 **Instead of forcing sharing, focus on turn-taking:**

👉 *"You can play with the truck for two minutes, then it's your friend's turn."*

🎮 **Use timers, visual cues, and praise to reinforce fair play.**

📖 **Biblical Example:** *God teaches us generosity over time—He doesn't expect instant perfection. Sharing is a learned skill, just like kindness and patience.* (2 Corinthians 9:7)

🌙 The Bedtime Procrastinator

Just as you're **ready to collapse,** your threenager **suddenly needs water, a story, and an existential discussion about dinosaurs.**

🛠️ **Fix:**

🎮 **Set a bedtime routine and stick to it:**

👉 **"One drink, one story, then lights out."**

🎮 **Use a visual bedtime chart** so they know what's coming next.

🎮 **Stay consistent—negotiating only fuels the delay tactics.**

📖 **Biblical Wisdom:** *Even God established rhythms of rest, because He knew we needed them!* (Psalm 127:2 – *"He grants sleep to those He loves."*)

 **Pro Tip: Structure, patience, and a sense of humour are your best weapons in this level.** You're shaping a little person who is learning boundaries, kindness, and self-control—one meltdown at a time.

📖 **Biblical Encouragement:** *"Let us not grow weary in doing good, for at the proper time we will reap a harvest if we do not give up." — Galatians 6:9*

Now go forth, **Player 1. The threenager years may be wild, but you are fully equipped for this battle!** 🚀✨

watch

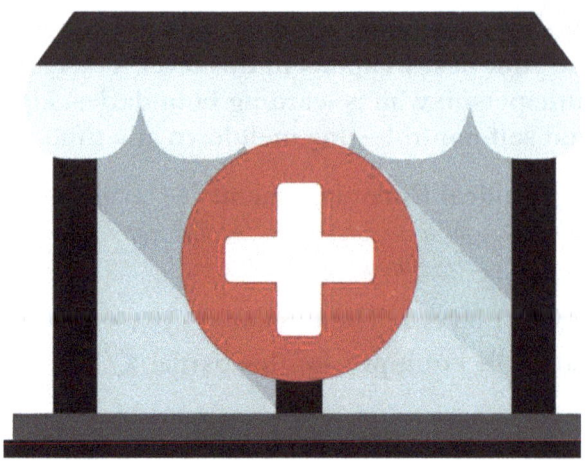

Cheat Codes for Level 3

Level 3 comes with **maxed-out emotions, unpredictable mood swings, and a toddler who thinks they run the world.** But don't worry—**you've got cheat codes!** These quick hacks will help **defuse meltdowns, encourage cooperation, and restore sanity (yours and theirs).**

📖 **Biblical Encouragement:** *Even in the wildest parenting moments, God equips you with wisdom, patience, and a little humor. (Proverbs 17:22 – "A cheerful heart is good medicine.")*

🎭 The Silly Distraction Buff

🔹 **Threenagers can't resist laughter.**

🔹 When things **start heading toward meltdown mode,** use:

🎮 **Silly voices** – "Uh-oh! The tickle monster is coming!"

🎮 **Exaggerated movements** – Pretend you're a clumsy giraffe getting dressed.

🎮 **Unexpected distractions** – Whisper, *"Hey, do you hear that? I think your teddy just said something!"*

📖 **Biblical Example:** *Even Jesus used unexpected, playful moments to shift focus and teach joyfully. (Matthew 18:3 – "Unless you change and become like little children, you will never enter the kingdom of heaven.")*

🍏 The Snack Negotiation Tactic

◆ **Snacks solve 80% of minor crises.**

◆ Keep a **stash of crackers, fruit, or raisins** to **prevent meltdowns before they start.**

◆ **Example:** "Let's sit and have a snack break, then we can try again."

📖 **Biblical Wisdom:** *God provides for our needs, often before we even realize them—sometimes, toddlers just need a little extra fuel. (Matthew 6:11 – "Give us this day our daily bread.")*

🌟 The Praise Power-Up

◆ **Catch them being good and celebrate it.**

◆ Reinforce positive behavior with **specific encouragement:**

🎮 "I love how you helped clean up your toys!"

🎮 "You waited so patiently—that was amazing!"

🎮 "Wow, I saw how kind you were to your friend. That made my heart happy."

📖 **Biblical Parallel:** *God encourages us by celebrating our progress, not just perfection. (Zephaniah 3:17 – "He will rejoice over you with singing.")*

Pro Tip: Threenagers **respond to joy, structure, and encouragement.** When things feel chaotic, **laugh, refuel, and build them up.**

📖 **Biblical Reminder:** *"Encourage one another and build each other up."* — 1 Thessalonians 5:11

Now go forth, **Player 1—use your cheat codes wisely, and may your snack stash never run dry!** 🚀✨

Save Point: The Magic of Storytime

Storytime isn't just about **books**—it's about **connection.** Whether you're snuggled on the couch, their head resting on your shoulder, or **bringing silly characters to life,** these moments **go beyond words on a page.**

📖 **Biblical Bonus:** *Jesus often used stories (parables) to teach deep truths in a way that engaged both hearts and minds. Storytelling isn't just entertaining—it's transformative. (Matthew 13:34)*

As you **read together,** you're not only **building their vocabulary and imagination** but also **showing them that your time and attention are fully theirs.** In a world full of distractions, this is a sacred pause—a chance to be fully present.

Why Storytime Matters

💛 **It creates a sanctuary.** Storytime **slows life down,** giving you both a moment to **breathe, bond, and recharge.**
💛 **It teaches life lessons.** Books about **bravery, kindness, and emotions** help your child **process their world** in a safe space.
💛 **It strengthens their faith.** Stories rooted in truth—whether

from **picture books or the Bible**—help lay a foundation of wisdom and wonder.

📖 **Biblical Parallel:** *God's Word is a lamp to our feet—it guides, comforts, and teaches. The stories we share with our children do the same. (Psalm 119:105)*

🎮 **Pro Tip:** 🛠️ Choose books that reflect their experiences and feelings.
📚 Stories about **bravery, friendship, and emotions** can help them **process challenges and triumphs.**
🎭 Use silly voices, ask questions, and make it interactive!

💡 And don't forget—**the greatest book you can ever introduce them to is God's Word.** Even simple Bible stories plant seeds of faith that will grow for a lifetime.

📖 *"Start children off on the way they should go, and even when they are old they will not turn from it." — Proverbs 22:6*

So grab a book, **make it silly, and savour the magic of being together.** These moments **are the real treasures of parenting.**
🎮💛✨

Side Quests!

These mini-missions aren't just for fun—they **build patience, creativity, and connection** while keeping your little one engaged. **Think of them as bonus XP for parenting!**

📖 **Biblical Encouragement:** *Jesus used everyday activities—like meals, walks, and storytelling—to teach, connect, and build relationships. These side quests may seem small, but they are powerful moments of growth.* (Deuteronomy 6:6-7)

🧱 BLOCK TOWER CHALLENGE

◆ **Objective:** Build the tallest block tower together.

◆ **How to Play:**

🎮 Take **turns adding blocks**, encouraging teamwork.

🎮 **Cheer them on** even when the tower topples.

🎮 **Celebrate effort over perfection.**

📖 **Biblical Wisdom:** *"Two are better than one, because they have a good return for their labor."* — Ecclesiastes 4:9

◆ **Reward: Encourages patience, teamwork, and a sense of achievement.** Plus, knocking it down is **half the fun!**

📖 STORY CREATOR MISSION

◆ **Objective:** Make up a **story together.**

◆ **How to Play:**

🎮 Take **turns adding a sentence** to build a story.

🎮 Act it out with **toys or puppets** for extra fun.

🎮 Draw pictures **to bring the story to life.**

📖 **Biblical Example:** *Jesus was the ultimate storyteller—His parables helped people understand deep truths. Stories help kids process their emotions and experiences, too!* (Matthew 13:34)

48

◆ **Reward: Boosts creativity, strengthens language skills, and gives you both a laugh.** (Bonus: You might discover your child is a storytelling genius!)

 Pro Tip: Side quests aren't **"just play"**—they're **building blocks for faith, learning, and connection.**

📖 **Biblical Encouragement:** *"Let all that you do be done in love."* — *1 Corinthians 16:14*

So, **Player 1, embrace the side quests!** Whether you're stacking blocks or spinning stories, **you're shaping a heart, not just passing time.** 🚀✨

 # Troubleshooting Guide

Issue	Fix
My child says "no" to everything, even things they want.	Stay calm and reframe requests as statements or fun challenges: "Time to race to the car!" or "Let's see if you can pick up your toys faster than me!"
They have constant tantrums over small things.	Acknowledge their feelings: "I see you're upset because your block tower fell." Redirect their focus or offer a simple solution to help them reset.
They won't share with siblings or friends.	Practice turn-taking instead of forcing sharing. "You can play with the car for two minutes, then it's your friend's turn."
They constantly interrupt conversations.	Teach them to wait their turn by introducing a simple signal (like holding your hand) to show they want to speak. Praise them when they succeed.
Bedtime takes forever because of stalling.	Keep bedtime routines consistent and set clear boundaries: "One story, then lights out." Use a timer to signal transitions.
They argue over every little thing.	Avoid power struggles by offering limited choices: "Do you want to wear the red shoes or the blue ones?" This gives them a sense of control.
They seem clingy or afraid to try new things.	Encourage small steps toward independence. Stay nearby to offer reassurance but celebrate their efforts when they take the initiative.
They whine instead of asking politely.	Model the behaviour you want to see. Gently prompt them: "Can you ask in a calm voice? Say, 'Can I have a snack, please?'"

Pro Tip for Troubleshooting

Threenagers are still learning to navigate their big feelings and growing independence. Your **calm, consistent guidance** teaches them that they're **safe to explore and express themselves—even when emotions run high.**

📖 **Biblical Reminder:** *"Be completely humble and gentle; be patient, bearing with one another in love." — Ephesians 4:2*

Now go forth, **Player 1. You're shaping their heart, not just their behavior.** 🚀 ✨

Level 4

The School Years (6-9 Years)

Congratulations, Player 1! You've Reached The School Years

Welcome to **Level 4: The School Years**, where your child embarks on quests for **knowledge, friendships, and independence.** This level introduces **new challenges** like navigating **social dynamics, homework battles, and the** occasional showdown with The Comparison Monster.

Your mission? **Guide your player toward confidence, resilience, and a lifelong love of learning—without losing your sanity.**

📖 **Biblical Encouragement:** *"Start children off on the way they should go, and even when they are old they will not turn from it."* — Proverbs 22:6

 Pro tip: The School Years **are a balance of structure and play.** Encourage exploration **while providing guardrails.** They'll thank you someday—**probably not today, though.**

Core Mission: Build Confidence and Resilience

At this stage, your child starts facing **"real-world" challenges**—from **understanding fractions** to **figuring out playground politics.** Your job is to be their **co-pilot**—offering **guidance while letting them take the controls.**

📖 **Biblical Parallel:** *Just as God walks with us through our challenges rather than removing them, we are called to guide our children without doing everything for them. (Isaiah 41:10)*

How to Build Confidence and Resilience

🛠 Celebrate Effort Over Results
◆ **Praise their hard work, not just their wins.**
◆ **Example:** "You worked so hard on that project—I'm proud of you! How do you feel about that?"

📖 **Biblical Wisdom:** *God values faithfulness over perfection. Encouraging effort over outcomes helps kids develop a growth mindset. (Colossians 3:23 – "Whatever you do, work at it with all your heart.")*

🛠 Let Them Solve Problems
◆ **Resist the urge to swoop in.**
◆ Instead of fixing everything, **ask guiding questions:**
🎮 *"What do you think you could do next?"*
🎮 *"What's another way to solve this?"*

📖 **Biblical Example:** *Jesus often answered questions with questions, teaching people to think critically and find solutions. (Luke 10:36 – "Which of these three do you think was a neighbor to the man who fell into the hands of robbers?")*

🛠 Teach Them to Fail Forward
◆ **Normalize mistakes as part of learning.**
◆ **Share your own failures** and what you learned from them.
◆ **Example:** *"I remember when I messed up at work—I learned that mistakes help us grow!"*

📖 **Biblical Wisdom:** *Failure isn't final—God uses it to shape us and build resilience. (Romans 5:3-4 – "Suffering produces perseverance; perseverance, character; and character, hope.")*

 Pro tip: Confidence **isn't about avoiding failure—it's about learning to bounce back.**

📖 **Biblical Encouragement:** *"For though the righteous fall seven times, they rise again." — Proverbs 24:16*

Now **press start, Player 1—Level 4 is full of adventure, and you are exactly the guide your child needs!** 🚀✨

Big Boss: The Homework Hydra

The **Homework Hydra** is a **multi-headed beast** that spawns **new challenges every night.** Just when you **think you've conquered maths,** it rears another head—**spelling lists, science projects, and reading logs.**

But fear not, Player 1! **You are not alone in this battle.** With the right strategy, **your child can learn to slay the Homework Hydra with confidence.**

📖 **Biblical Encouragement:** *"Commit to the Lord whatever you do, and He will establish your plans."* — Proverbs 16:3

Defeat Strategy

🛡 **Create a Homework Zone**

◆ **Set up a distraction-free space** stocked with all the supplies they need.

◆ **Make it comfortable but structured.** (Bonus points for snacks!)

📖 **Biblical Wisdom:** *Even Jesus sought quiet places for important tasks—setting up a designated space helps kids focus. (Mark 1:35)*

🛡️ Break It Down
◆ **One head at a time.** The **Homework Hydra thrives on overwhelm,** so tackle it piece by piece.

◆ **Example:** *"Let's do 10 minutes of reading, then take a break."*

📖 **Biblical Wisdom:** *Jesus taught step by step, using parables and lessons in manageable pieces. Learning is a journey, not a sprint! (Matthew 13:31-32)*

🛡️ Offer Support, Not Solutions
◆ **Guide them, but let them do the work.**
◆ **Encouraging words:**

🎮 *"I'm here if you need help, but I know you've got this!"*

🎮 *"Try thinking through the problem—what do you already know?"*

📖 **Biblical Wisdom:** *God equips us for our challenges rather than just removing them. Learning to persevere builds strength. (James 1:5)*

Pro tip: Avoid making **homework battles about you.** It's their quest, not yours. Your job? **Be the wise mentor—not the knight doing the battle for them.**

📖 **Biblical Encouragement:** *"Train up a child in the way they should go, and when they are old, they will not depart from it."* — Proverbs 22:6

So **gear up, Player 1.** The **Homework Hydra is fierce,** but with patience, strategy, and the right encouragement, **your child will learn to slay it—one challenge at a time!** 🚀📚✨

Gameplay Hazards

The School Years **introduce new challenges,** from social pressures to forgotten lunchboxes. **But fear not, Player 1!** These hazards are just side quests, and with the right strategies, **you and your child can navigate them like pros.**

📖 **Biblical Encouragement:** *"The Lord makes firm the steps of the one who delights in Him." — Psalm 37:23*

🐯 The Comparison Monster

This sneaky villain **lurks at learner conversations, birthday parties, and school award nights,** whispering that your child should be **smarter, faster, or better at piano than their peers.**

🛠 Fix:
🎮 Focus on your child's unique strengths and celebrate **their** progress.
🎮 Remind them (and yourself!) that everyone **levels up at their own pace.**

58

📋 **Biblical Truth:** *God created each of us uniquely, with different gifts and callings. The only person we need to compare ourselves to is who we were yesterday.* (Psalm 139:14)

🤦 The "I Forgot" Glitch

Lost homework? Forgotten lunches? Shoes mysteriously missing before school? This glitch is **part of the game.**

🛠️ **Fix:**

🎮 **Teach them to use tools** like **calendars, checklists, or reminder apps** to build responsibility.

🎮 **Make it fun!** A **"morning checklist" challenge** can turn routine tasks into a game.

📋 **Biblical Wisdom:** *Even God gives us reminders to help us stay on track!* (Deuteronomy 6:6-9 – *"Tie them as symbols on your hands and bind them on your foreheads."*)

😨 The FOMO Goblin (Fear of Missing Out)

FOMO hits hard when every friend seems to have **the latest gadget, coolest camp, or trendiest shoes.**

🛠️ **Fix:**

🎮 **Set boundaries around wants vs. needs.** *"I know you really want that game console, but let's save up for it together."*

🎮 **Teach contentment** by modeling gratitude and showing them that **true joy doesn't come from stuff.**

📋 **Biblical Wisdom:** *"Life does not consist in an abundance of possessions."* — Luke 12:15

🏫 The School Choice Showdown

Public? Private? Homeschool? Alternative? **Debates over school choices can feel overwhelming,** leaving you doubting your decisions.

🛠️ **Fix:**

🎮 The "best" school is the one that fits your child's needs and your family's values.

🎮 Tour schools, meet teachers, and focus on environments where your child will feel supported.

🎮 Trust that God can guide and provide, no matter where they learn.

📖 **Reassurance:** *No school is perfect, but your involvement as a parent has a bigger impact than any institution.*

"If any of you lacks wisdom, you should ask God, who gives generously to all without finding fault." — James 1:5

 Pro Tip: You're not locked into one path—**stay adaptable.** No matter the hazard, **your steady presence is what matters most.**

📖 **Biblical Encouragement:** *"For I know the plans I have for you," declares the Lord, "plans to prosper you and not to harm you, plans to give you hope and a future." — Jeremiah 29:11*

Now **press start, Player 1.** The School Years **may come with new challenges, but you've got the ultimate guide—God's wisdom and your own loving heart.** 🚀✨

watch

60

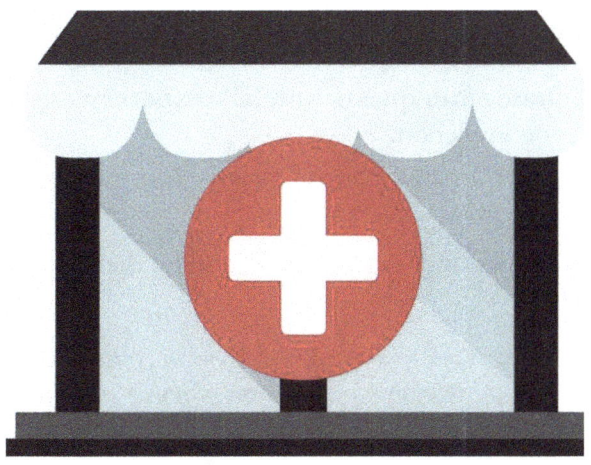

Cheat Codes for Level 4

The **School Years** come with **new responsibilities, busier schedules, and higher-level parenting challenges.** But don't worry—**these cheat codes will help keep your family connected, motivated, and well-rested!**

📖 **Biblical Encouragement:** *"Let us not become weary in doing good, for at the proper time we will reap a harvest if we do not give up."* — *Galatians 6:9*

🛡️ Family Meeting Power-Up

🔹 **Weekly check-ins** help **everyone stay on the same page** about schedules, goals, and responsibilities.

🔹 **Use this time** to celebrate wins, solve challenges, and make sure no one feels overwhelmed.

🔹 **Bonus:** It models **teamwork and problem-solving**, which kids will use for life.

📖 **Biblical Example:** *Jesus regularly gathered His disciples to teach, check in, and strengthen their faith—because unity matters! (Mark 9:30-31)*

🖌️ Gamify Chores

◆ **Turn chores into quests** with **XP (experience points) rewards** for completion.

🎮 *"Clean your room to earn 50 XP toward an ice cream outing!"*

🎮 *"Help with dinner? 25 XP bonus!"*

◆ **Track points on a simple chart** and let them "level up" for small rewards.

📖 **Biblical Parallel:** *Even in Scripture, work is tied to joy and reward. (Colossians 3:23 – "Whatever you do, work at it with all your heart, as working for the Lord.")*

🌙 Bedtime Wind-Down Ritual

◆ **Create a calming bedtime routine** to help kids **process their day and build connection.**

◆ **Ideas:**

📖 Reading a short Bible story or favorite book.

💬 Talking about **highs & lows** of their day.

🙏 Sharing **three things they're grateful for.**

📖 **Biblical Encouragement:** *Ending the day in gratitude helps shift focus from stress to God's goodness. (1 Thessalonians 5:16-18 – "Rejoice always, pray continually, give thanks in all circumstances.")*

🎮 **Pro Tip:** These cheat codes aren't just **parenting hacks**—they're ways to **build stronger relationships and shape your child's heart.**

📖 **Biblical Reminder:** *"Train up a child in the way they should go, and when they are old they will not turn from it."* — Proverbs 22:6

Now go forth, **Player 1. Equip your family with these power-ups, and may your XP points always lead to more joy!**
🚀✨

Save Point: Family Dinners That Actually Happen

Life is busy. **Between school, work, and activities, sitting down for a meal together can feel like an impossible quest.** But even **once or twice a week**, family meals act like a **reset button**—a chance to **slow down, connect, and be fully present.**

📖 **Biblical Encouragement:** *Jesus often connected with people over meals, using that time for teaching, encouragement, and relationship-building. Sharing a table is a sacred act of love and connection. (Luke 24:30-31)*

Why Family Dinners Matter

💛 **They create a pause in the chaos.** Even a quick meal **grounds your family, offering a moment of peace and togetherness.**

💛 **They foster conversation.** Whether it's **a goofy story, a vent about homework, or a deep question,** mealtime gives kids a space to **be heard.**

💛 **They remind your child they belong.** Your table is **more than a place to eat—it's a place of security, love, and shared memories.**

📖 **Biblical Example:** *Jesus fed the five thousand—not just to provide food, but to bring people together in community and trust. (John 6:1-13)*

How to Make It Work

🍱 **Breakfast counts!** If dinner is impossible, **share a quick morning meal together.**

🍕 **Takeout still counts!** It's not about homemade perfection—it's about presence.

 Make it fun! Try **conversation starters**, a **"best and worst part of your day"** check-in, or **a gratitude round.**

📖 **Biblical Encouragement:** *"How good and pleasant it is when God's people live together in unity!"* — Psalm 133:1

🎮 **Pro Tip: Keep it simple.** It's **not about the food—it's about the connection. Every shared meal is a tiny victory in the game of family life.**

Now go forth, **Player 1,** and enjoy the moments around the table. **Even the messy, chaotic ones—they're all part of the journey.** 🚀✨

Side Quests!

Not all learning happens in a classroom—**some of the best lessons come from shared experiences, teamwork, and play.** These **side quests** build **confidence, creativity, and connection** while making family life **a little more fun.**

📖 **Biblical Encouragement:** *"Encourage one another and build each other up." — 1 Thessalonians 5:11*

📚 HOMEWORK HELPER GUILD

◆ **Objective:** Support your child during homework time.

◆ **How to Play:**

🎮 Sit with them as a **study ally, not a micromanager.**

🎮 Ask **questions** to help them think through problems.

🎮 **Encourage effort** rather than just correct mistakes.

📖 **Biblical Parallel:** *Jesus walked alongside His disciples, guiding them without taking over their journey. Your role is to support, not control. (Luke 24:15-16)*

◆ **Reward: Builds their confidence and reinforces that learning is a team effort.** Plus, it **keeps the Homework Hydra from growing extra heads!** 🐉📚

🎲 DIY GAME NIGHT

◆ **Objective: Create a simple board game together.**

◆ **How to Play:**

🎮 Use **paper, pencils, and dice** to invent a game with your own rules.

🎮 Make it **fun and flexible**—let your child lead!

🎮 Play as a family and **tweak the rules as you go.**

📖 **Biblical Parallel:** *God delights in creativity, and play is a way to celebrate joy, imagination, and togetherness. (Genesis 1:31 – "And God saw all that He had made, and it was very good.")*

🔷 **Reward:** Encourages **creativity, problem-solving, and teamwork**—plus, it's **a great way to bond as a family.**

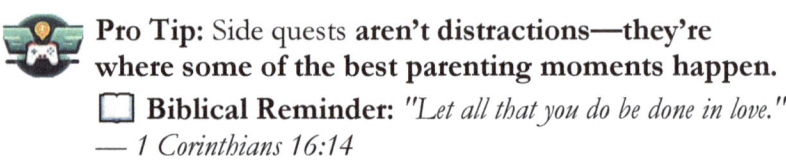 **Pro Tip:** Side quests **aren't distractions—they're where some of the best parenting moments happen.**
📖 **Biblical Reminder:** *"Let all that you do be done in love."* — 1 Corinthians 16:14

Now go forth, **Player 1. Whether you're tackling homework or rolling the dice in a homemade game, you're building something greater—memories that last.** 🚀✨

Troubleshooting Guide

Issue	Fix
My child refuses to do homework.	Break tasks into smaller chunks and offer short breaks between. Use positive reinforcement: "Once this is done, we can play your favourite game!"
They compare themselves to others.	Highlight their unique strengths and focus on effort over results: "You worked so hard on that project—I'm so proud of you!"
They resist helping with chores.	Turn chores into games or use incentives like sticker charts: "Let's see how fast we can pick up the toys!"
They struggle to make friends at school.	Role-play common social situations and teach them conversation starters: "Hi, can I play with you?"
They won't put down screens to join family activities.	Set clear screen-time limits and create screen-free zones, like during meals or family time. Offer engaging alternatives like a family board game.
They complain about being bored all the time.	Encourage creativity by suggesting open-ended activities like building with blocks or drawing. Let them know it's okay to feel bored sometimes—it sparks creativity.
They struggle with losing games or competitions.	Model good sportsmanship and emphasize the fun of playing, not just winning. Praise their effort and teamwork.
They are afraid to try new activities.	Start small and offer encouragement: "I know it feels scary, but let's try it together." Celebrate their bravery, even if they only take the first step.

Pro Tip for Troubleshooting

The **School Years** aren't just about academics—they're about **building confidence, resilience, and character.**

✅ **Celebrate their small wins.** Every step forward—big or small—is progress worth cheering.

✅ **Guide them through challenges.** Let them struggle *just enough* to learn perseverance, but remind them they're never alone.

✅ **Reinforce their true worth.** Their value isn't measured by grades, trophies, or achievements—it comes from **who they are** and **who God made them to be.**

📖 **Biblical Encouragement:** *"I praise You because I am fearfully and wonderfully made; Your works are wonderful, I know that full well."* — *Psalm 139:14*

In a world that pushes performance, teach them that they are loved for simply being them. 💛

Now go forth, **Player 1—equip your child with confidence, faith, and the courage to keep leveling up!** 🚀✨

Level 5

The Tween Years (10-12 Years)

Congratulations, Player 1! You've Reached The Tween Years, a bridge between **childhood and the teenage gauntlet**. This stage is packed with **budding independence, heightened curiosity, and, yes, a bit of sass.**

Your mission? **Help your tween navigate this transitional time with confidence while keeping the lines of connection strong.**

☐ **Biblical Encouragement:** *"Be completely humble and gentle; be patient, bearing with one another in love." — Ephesians 4:2*

What to Expect in This Level

◆ **Tweens are figuring out who they are.** They're testing boundaries, exploring new interests, and **starting to care deeply about what their peers think.**

◆ **They may pretend they don't need you—but they do.** Your role shifts from **"leader of the game" to co-op teammate.**

◆ **Connection happens in the in-between moments.** Tweens often **open up unexpectedly**—while folding laundry, driving, or gaming together.

☐ **Biblical Reminder:** *Even when we try to "go solo," God is always there, ready to guide us back to Him. Your steady presence mirrors this kind of love. (Deuteronomy 31:8)*

Core Mission: Building Independence While Staying Connected

Tweens are **starting to seek independence,** but they **still need you as their anchor.** Your job is to **give them room to explore** while **keeping them tethered to the values and support systems that will guide them through tougher levels ahead.**

70

📖 **Biblical Wisdom:** *"Train up a child in the way they should go, and when they are old, they will not turn from it."* — Proverbs 22:6

✅ **Let them make small decisions.** When they feel ownership over choices (like how to organize their room or pick their extracurriculars), they build confidence.

✅ **Be their safe base, not their micromanager.** Connection **doesn't mean controlling**—it means being their go-to person when they need advice, reassurance, or a **reminder of who they are.**

✅ **Celebrate effort, not just results.** *"I'm proud of how much work you put into that project"* builds resilience, even when things don't go perfectly.

📖 **Biblical Encouragement:** *"Let us not grow weary in doing good, for at the proper time we will reap a harvest if we do not give up."* — Galatians 6:9

 Pro tip: Tweens often open up in unexpected moments. Instead of forcing conversations, create space for natural ones—**while driving, playing games, or cooking together.** These quiet, casual moments **often lead to the most important talks.**

Now go forth, **Player 1. You are the co-op teammate they need—even if they pretend they don't!** 🚀✨

Big Boss Battle: The Peer Pressure Phantom

The **Peer Pressure Phantom** is a sneaky boss that thrives in the **shadows of insecurity and the desire to fit in.** It whispers lies like, *"You need to change to be accepted,"* or *"Everyone else is doing it, so you should too."* Whether it's about **joining social media, wearing the "right" clothes, or trying something they're not ready for,** this boss feeds on your tween's fear of standing out.

But you, Player 1, have the tools to help them **stay grounded in their values and confident in who they are.**

📖 **Biblical Truth:** *"Do not conform to the pattern of this world, but be transformed by the renewing of your mind."* — Romans 12:2

Defeat Strategy

🛡 **1. Equip Them with Tools**

🔷 Teach them **how to say no with confidence.**

🔷 **Role-play scenarios** where they might feel pressure—practice responses together so they're ready when it counts.

🔷 Help them understand that saying *no* doesn't mean losing friends—it means **staying true to themselves.**

📖 *"Let your yes be yes and your no be no."* — Matthew 5:37

🛡 2. Talk About It Before It Happens

◆ **Have open conversations** about peer pressure before they face it.

◆ Share **age-appropriate stories** from your own life—times you felt pressured and how you responded.

◆ Let them know that **everyone—even adults—face peer pressure at times.**

📖 **Biblical Wisdom:** *"Plans fail for lack of counsel, but with many advisers they succeed." — Proverbs 15:22*

🛡 3. Reinforce Their Strengths

◆ Celebrate their **unique qualities, values, and interests.**

◆ Remind them that **God created them with purpose and intention.**

◆ Help them build **identity and self-worth that isn't based on popularity or likes.**

📖 *"You are God's masterpiece, created in Christ Jesus to do good works." — Ephesians 2:10*

Pro Tip: When your tween is **overwhelmed by social pressure**, your **calm, steady response** helps them reset. Avoid escalating the drama—**be the safe place they need.**

📖 *"A gentle answer turns away wrath, but a harsh word stirs up anger." — Proverbs 15:1*

Now go forth, **Player 1.** With your guidance, your tween can face the **Peer Pressure Phantom** with courage, clarity, and conviction.

🛡✨

Gameplay Hazards

This level introduces **complex social dynamics, shifting motivation, and emotional rollercoasters.** But don't panic—these **gameplay hazards** are common, and with the right strategies, you can help your tween **build resilience, responsibility, and self-worth.**

📖 **Biblical Encouragement:** *"The Lord is close to the brokenhearted and saves those who are crushed in spirit."* — Psalm 34:18

🌀 The Drama Cyclone
Friendship conflicts can spiral quickly over minor issues, leaving your tween feeling **hurt, confused, or isolated.**

🛠️ **Fix:**

🎮 Teach them to **pause and process** emotions before reacting.

🎮 Help them **see multiple perspectives**—what did their friend feel, and why?

🎮 Practice **calm, constructive ways** to resolve conflict and repair relationships.

📖 **Biblical Parallel:** *"Everyone should be quick to listen, slow to speak and slow to become angry."* — James 1:19

👾 The Motivation Gremlin

Your tween may avoid responsibilities like **homework or chores** in favour of **easier, more enjoyable distractions** (hello, YouTube and Minecraft).

🛠 Fix:

🎮 **Break tasks into smaller steps** to make them manageable.

🎮 Use **challenges, timers, or mini rewards** to gamify tasks.

🎮 Reinforce **effort over outcome** with genuine encouragement.

📖 *"Whatever you do, work at it with all your heart, as working for the Lord."* — *Colossians 3:23*

💔 The Confidence Crusher

Tweens often **compare themselves to others**, especially online, which can lead to **self-doubt and lowered self-esteem**.

🛠 Fix:

🎮 Focus on their **God-given strengths and unique gifts.**

🎮 Teach them that **social media highlights aren't real life**—and that real value isn't based on appearance, popularity, or followers.

🎮 Affirm their identity regularly: *"You are kind, creative, and deeply loved just as you are."*

📖 *"People look at the outward appearance, but the Lord looks at the heart."* — *1 Samuel 16:7*

 Pro Tip: These years can feel like emotional whiplash, but your tween's wild reactions are **a sign of growth**, not failure. **Your steady, loving presence is the ultimate stabilizer.**

Now go forth, **Player 1**—the tween years may be stormy, but you've got the tools, the wisdom, and the heart to guide them through every hazard. 🚀 💛

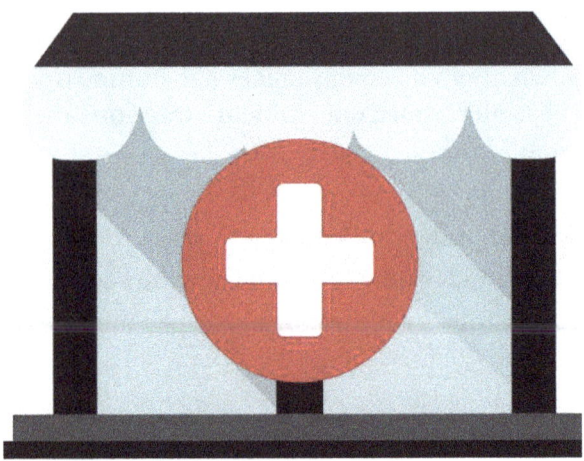

Level 5 is all about **building trust, independence, and emotional intelligence.** Your tween is starting to think more deeply, question more boldly, and crave both **freedom and connection.** These cheat codes help you meet them where they are—and **keep the relationship strong** as they navigate this critical stage.

📖 **Biblical Encouragement:** *"Fathers [and mothers], do not exasperate your children; instead, bring them up in the training and instruction of the Lord." — Ephesians 6:4*

💬 **Ask for Their Opinions**

◆ Get their input on **family decisions**, like planning a weekend outing, choosing a new recipe to try, or picking a family movie.

◆ Involve them in conversations that matter—it helps them feel **valued, capable, and heard.**

◆ Bonus: This builds **critical thinking and problem-solving skills.**

📖 *"The purposes of a person's heart are deep waters, but one who has insight draws them out." — Proverbs 20:5*

🔁 **Normalize Mistakes**

◆ Share **your own missteps** (age-appropriate ones!) and how you worked through them.

◆ This helps them see that **failure isn't final—it's feedback.**

◆ It also gives them **permission to be human** and take healthy risks.

📖 *"Though the righteous fall seven times, they rise again." — Proverbs 24:16*

🔲 **Tech-Free Time Together**

◆ Set aside **regular "no devices" zones**, like during meals, car rides, or bedtime routines.

◆ Use this time for **talking, laughing, or just being together** without screens in the way.

◆ These tech-free moments become the **relational glue** that holds everything else together.

📖 *"Be still, and know that I am God." — Psalm 46:10*

 Pro Tip: Tween connection isn't about **big lectures or perfect parenting**—it's about **consistent, meaningful moments** that show: *"I see you. I value you. I'm here for you."*

Now go forth, **Player 1**—you're raising a wise, resilient, and deeply loved human being, one cheat code at a time. 🚀💛

Save Point: Traditions and Check-ins

As your tween begins to explore the world with **growing independence**, it's easy to feel them pulling away. But even as they stretch, **they crave stability and connection** more than they let on.

Save Points in this level aren't about control—they're about creating rituals that remind them they are safe, known, and loved.

> 📖 **Biblical Encouragement:** *"These commandments that I give you today are to be on your hearts. Impress them on your children. Talk about them when you sit at home..."* — Deuteronomy 6:6–7

Simple Traditions That Make a Big Impact

💛 **Weekly Rituals:**
✓ Sunday pancakes,
✓ Friday movie nights,
✓ Taco Tuesdays—whatever fits your family vibe.

💬 **Daily Check-Ins:**

✓ A quick *"What was the best part of your day?"*

✓ Or a "High/Low" conversation before bed.

These moments become **anchors**, grounding your tween in the knowledge that **no matter how big their world gets, your connection remains steady.**

📖 *"He will be the sure foundation for your times, a rich store of salvation and wisdom and knowledge."* — Isaiah 33:6

Pro Tip: Help your tween **build emotional resilience** by encouraging them to **pause before reacting**—whether it's to friendship drama, school stress, or a frustrating situation.

💬 Teach them simple questions to ask themselves like:

👉 "How big is this problem really?"

👉 "What would help me calm down before I respond?"

📖 *"A person's wisdom yields patience; it is to one's glory to overlook an offense."* — Proverbs 19:11

These small, consistent check-ins aren't just routines—**they're sacred rhythms** that build trust, emotional strength, and lifelong connection.

Now go forth, **Player 1.** These Save Points might seem ordinary—but they're building something extraordinary. 💛🎮

Side Quests!

Tween years are the perfect time for **intentional bonding through shared challenges and creative play.** These **Side Quests** build communication, confidence, and connection—while keeping things fun and low-pressure.

📖 **Biblical Encouragement:** *"Two are better than one, because they have a good return for their labor." — Ecclesiastes 4:9*

👤 FAMILY DEBATE NIGHT

◆ **Objective:** Spark critical thinking and respectful dialogue.
◆ **How to Play:**
🎮 Choose light-hearted topics like:
- *"Which is the best pet: dog or dragon?"*
- *"Is cereal a soup?"*

  🎮 Give everyone 1–2 minutes to share their argument—no interruptions!

  🎮 Bonus points for creativity, logic, and humor.

◆ **Reward:**
✓ Builds **confidence in expressing opinions**
✓ Strengthens **listening and reasoning skills**
✓ Turns conversation into connection

📖 *"Let your conversation be always full of grace, seasoned with salt, so that you may know how to answer everyone." — Colossians 4:6*

🎨 SHARED CREATIVE PROJECT

◆ **Objective:** Work together on a meaningful, long-term project.

◆ **How to Play:**

🎮 Pick something to build or create together—like:
- A **family photo album or scrapbook**
- A **DIY craft or LEGO masterpiece**
- A **short comic, podcast, or stop-motion video**

◆ **Reward:**

✓ Encourages **teamwork and creativity**

✓ Gives your tween a sense of **ownership and pride**

✓ Creates lasting **memories and conversation starters**

📖 *"He has filled them with skill to do all kinds of work... all of them skilled workers and designers." — Exodus 35:35*

 **Pro Tip:** These side quests might feel simple, but they are **secret weapons** for building trust and deepening your relationship.

You're not just spending time—you're investing in their growth. 💛✨

Now go forth, **Player 1—unlock those hidden side quests, and have fun doing it!** 🚀

Troubleshooting Guide

Issue	Fix
They don't talk to me as much.	Create low-pressure moments for connection, like car rides or cooking together. Avoid grilling them with questions—let them come to you naturally.
They seem obsessed with fitting in.	Reinforce their individuality by celebrating their unique traits. Share stories of times when staying true to yourself worked in your favour.
They're glued to their devices.	Set clear boundaries for screen time and enforce "tech-free" family moments. Model healthy tech habits yourself to lead by example.
They roll their eyes at everything I say.	Don't take it personally—it's often a tween's way of asserting independence. Respond with humour or empathy to keep the connection alive.
They're always comparing themselves to others.	Help them focus on their personal strengths and successes. Discuss how social media often portrays a filtered, unrealistic version of life.
Friendship drama takes over their life.	Teach them to pause before reacting and encourage open communication with friends. Help them see conflicts from multiple perspectives.
They avoid responsibility.	Break tasks into smaller steps and offer positive reinforcement for completing them. Make it fun by turning chores into challenges or competitions.
They struggle with self-esteem.	Remind them of their accomplishments and encourage them to try new things.

	Avoid over-praising and focus on effort over results.

 Pro Tip for Troubleshooting

Tweens are learning how to **stand on their own**, but they still need your **presence, patience, and quiet support.**
Stay **available without hovering, interested without interrogating**, and **supportive without solving everything for them.**

📖 *"Encourage one another and build each other up."* — *1 Thessalonians 5:11*

Your steady presence is the **anchor that helps them brave the waves of change.** Keep showing up, Player 1—**you're doing holy work, one conversation at a time.** 💛🚀

watch

Level 6

The Teen Years (13-18 Years)

Welcome to **Level 6: The Teen Years**, where your child evolves into a **highly skilled, fiercely independent, and occasionally eye-rolling master of sarcasm**. This level is a **tricky balance**—giving them the space to grow while staying emotionally connected in a world full of digital distractions.

Your primary mission? **Maintain real connection**, guide them through **complex emotional and social terrain**, and equip them with the tools they need to **level up to adulthood**.

📖 **Biblical Encouragement:** *"Let us not love with words or speech but with actions and in truth."* — 1 John 3:18

 Pro tip: Teenagers don't need you to fix everything—they need you to **listen, respect their growing autonomy**, and remind them you're **always in their corner**.

Even when they act like they don't care, **your presence still matters**. Probably more than they'll admit.

Core Mission: Prioritise Real Connection Over Virtual Noise

Teens are **hyper-connected online** but often feel **disconnected in real life**. Your challenge is to **compete with the noise of screens and scrolls**—not by demanding attention, but by offering presence, trust, and intentional engagement.

📖 *"Be quick to listen, slow to speak, and slow to become angry."* — James 1:19

85

How to Build Real Connection

🛠 1. Be Present Without Hovering
◆ Show up for **the big things**—sports games, recitals, birthdays, late-night heart-to-hearts.

◆ Give them **space to make choices, even mistakes.**

◆ Let them know: *"I'm here when you need me."*

🛠 2. Model Healthy Screen Habits
◆ Your teen is watching you more than you think.

◆ If you're always on your phone, they'll think that's normal.

◆ Create **device-free spaces** like:

✓ Family dinners

✓ Car rides

✓ Sunday mornings

📖 *"Set an example for the believers in speech, in conduct, in love, in faith and in purity."* — 1 Timothy 4:12

🛠 3. Ask Open-Ended Questions
◆ Move beyond *"How was school?"* to questions that open the door:
- *"What's something that made you laugh today?"*
- *"What's your favourite part of that game you're into?"*
- *"What's something you wish adults understood better about being a teen?"*

◆ And then—**listen. Don't fix. Don't preach. Just listen.**

Teenagers live in a hyper-connected world, but ironically, that often leads to disconnection. Social media, devices, and online games compete for their attention, but nothing replaces real, face-to-face connection. Your challenge is to stay relevant and engaged in their lives without invading their growing independence.

How to build real connection:

1. **Be Present Without Hovering:**
     - Show up for the important stuff—sports games, performances, late-night chats—but give them space to be themselves.
2. **Model Healthy Screen Habits:**
     - Teens will mimic what they see. If you're glued to your phone, they will be too. Create device-free zones like family dinners or car rides.
3. **Ask Open-Ended Questions:**
     - Move beyond "How was school?" and try, "What's something interesting that happened today?" or "What's your favourite thing about that game you're playing?"

 Pro tip: The moments they **finally open up** may not be convenient—they'll happen in the hallway, at 10:43 p.m., or during a random car ride.

Be ready to **pause your plans and lean in**—those moments are gold.

📖 *"The wise in heart are called discerning, and gracious words promote instruction." — Proverbs 16:21*

Now go forth, **Player 1.** You're parenting a teenager—and though the level is harder, the rewards are richer. You've got what it takes. 💛 🚀

Listen

Big Boss Battle: The Eye Roll Master

Ah yes, the **Eye Roll Master**—a formidable foe that appears whenever you offer advice, make a dad joke, or *simply exist*. This boss wields **sarcasm, dramatic sighs**, and a **supernatural ability to make you question your parenting confidence.**

But take heart, Player 1—this is **a classic teen defence mechanism, not a final boss.** With strategy and grace, you can navigate these encounters and keep your connection intact.

📖 **Biblical Wisdom:** *"A gentle answer turns away wrath, but a harsh word stirs up anger."* — *Proverbs 15:1*

Defeat Strategy

🛡 1. Don't Take It Personally

◆ Eye rolls and snark are usually signs of **internal frustration, insecurity, or overwhelm**—not a rejection of you.

◆ Remind yourself: *"This is not about me."*

📖 *Even God's people rolled their eyes at Him, and He responded with patience and love. (Exodus 16:2–4)*

🛡️ 2. Stay Curious

◆ Instead of snapping back, try: *"That's an interesting take—tell me more."*

◆ Curiosity **diffuses tension** and helps your teen feel **heard, not managed.**

◆ It also buys you time to **choose wisdom over reaction.**

🛡️ 3. Pick Your Battles

◆ Focus on **core values** like respect, safety, and integrity.

◆ Let minor things—like fashion choices, dramatic sighs, or messy hair—slide when you can.

◆ Save your energy for **what really matters.**

📖 *"Above all else, guard your heart, for everything you do flows from it."* — *Proverbs 4:23*

Pro Tip: Humour is your secret weapon.
A well-timed joke, playful comeback, or shared meme might just **crack the armour of teenage sarcasm** and earn you a **reluctant smile—or even a laugh.**

📖 *"A cheerful heart is good medicine."* — *Proverbs 17:22*

Now go forth, **Player 1.** The Eye Roll Master may challenge your patience, but with love, humour, and perspective, **you'll win more battles than you think.** 🏆 💛

Gameplay Hazards

The Teen Years come with **increasing freedom**, but also **heightened risks**—especially when it comes to digital life, peer influence, and identity. These hazards aren't just distractions—they're **shaping how your teen sees themselves and the world.** But fear not, Player 1: **you're equipped to guide them through.**

📖 **Biblical Encouragement:** *"Be alert and of sober mind. Your enemy the devil prowls around like a roaring lion looking for someone to devour."* — *1 Peter 5:8*
(*Translation: Stay aware and intentional—it matters.*)

💰 The Social Media Siren
This seductive villain **draws teens in with endless scrolling, comparison traps, and the quest for likes.** It's shiny and addictive—but it often leaves them feeling **less-than.**

🛠️ **Fix:**

🎮 Talk openly about how **social media is curated, not real life.**

🎮 Encourage breaks and digital detoxes: *"It's okay to unplug—it*

90

doesn't mean you're missing out."

🎮 Remind them that **God values the unseen, not the filtered.**

📖 *"People look at the outward appearance, but the Lord looks at the heart." — 1 Samuel 16:7*

👤 The Peer Pressure Phantom
This shadowy figure **feeds on FOMO and the fear of not fitting in.** It whispers, *"Everyone else is doing it—why not you?"*
🛠 Fix:
🎮 Help them **trust their inner compass.**

🎮 **Role-play social scenarios** so they're ready to respond with confidence and tact.

🎮 Reinforce that **courage is doing what's right, even when it's hard.**

📖 *"Do not be misled: 'Bad company corrupts good character.'" — 1 Corinthians 15:33*

👾 The Device Addiction Gremlin
This sneaky gremlin **creeps into every corner of life**, turning texts, games, and DMs into **time vacuums** that crowd out rest, connection, and real-life joy.
🛠 Fix:
🎮 Set clear, consistent **screen time boundaries** (and stick to them).

🎮 Encourage **non-digital hobbies** like music, sport, journaling, or volunteering.

🎮 Model tech balance—**they're watching how you use your phone, too.**

📖 *"Everything is permissible for me—but not everything is beneficial." — 1 Corinthians 6:12*

Pro Tip: Digital distractions and peer pressure are loud—but your steady voice, quiet presence, and consistent values speak louder over time.

Be the calm in their chaos. **You're the player they still trust— even when the game gets intense.** 💛 🚀

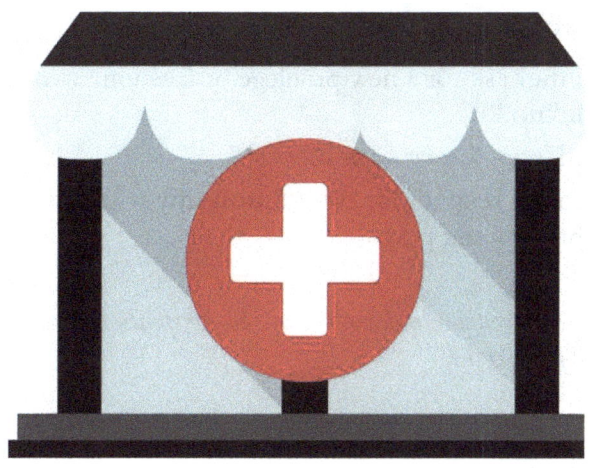

Cheat Codes for Level 6

This level is all about **coaching more than controlling, listening more than lecturing, and walking beside more than pushing from behind.** Your teen is learning to stretch their wings—and these cheat codes help you **stay connected while giving them space to grow.**

📖 **Biblical Encouragement:** *"Fathers [and mothers], do not provoke your children to anger, but bring them up in the discipline and instruction of the Lord." — Ephesians 6:4*

🚗 The Car Ride Confessional
◆ Teens often feel more comfortable opening up **when there's no pressure or eye contact**—cue the power of the car ride.
◆ Ask open-ended questions and let silence breathe.
◆ Even if the convo seems random, **lean in—it could be gold.**

📖 *Jesus often connected deeply during long walks or shared journeys—real talk happens on the move. (Luke 24:13–32)*

💬 The "Yes" Buffer
◆ When they ask for a new privilege or freedom, **avoid the knee-jerk "no."**
◆ Instead, say: *"Let me think about it."*
◆ This shows **respect for their autonomy** while giving you space to process and pray.

📖 *"Everyone should be quick to listen, slow to speak and slow to become angry."* — James 1:19

🛠️ The Fail-Safe Reaction
◆ When they **mess up (and they will)**, focus on **restoring, not just correcting.**
◆ Ask: *"What can we do to fix this?"*
◆ This promotes **ownership, problem-solving, and trust.**

📖 *"The Lord is gracious and compassionate, slow to anger and rich in love."* — Psalm 145:8

 Pro Tip: Your **calm, consistent, grace-filled approach** creates a safe space for your teen to learn from their mistakes and keep growing. **You're not just raising a kid—you're launching a future adult.**

Now go forth, **Player 1.** The terrain may be tougher, but your toolkit is stronger than ever. Keep playing the long game—you're doing holy work. 💛🚀

watch

Save Point: Car Rides with Unexpected Honesty

There's something **quietly magical** about the car. No eye contact, no pressure, no immediate escape—just the hum of the road and space to breathe.

For teens, this often becomes a **sacred space to open up.** It's where the truth sneaks out in between songs, or after a long pause when you least expect it. These **Save Points** are rarely scheduled, but they're **worth everything.**

📖 **Biblical Encouragement:** *"Everyone should be quick to listen, slow to speak and slow to become angry." — James 1:19*

How to Make the Most of This Save Point

◆ **Truly Listen:**
Be present. Let go of the urge to **interrupt, fix, or advise.** Sometimes they don't need solutions—just **space to be heard.**

◆ **Let Silence Be Okay:**
The quiet isn't awkward—it's **room for thought.** Your calm presence speaks volumes.

◆ **Ask Gently, Not Grilling:**

Try open-ended prompts like:
- *"What was the highlight of your day?"*
- *"How are things with your friends lately?"*
- *"What do you think about [insert current topic]?"*

 Jesus often used thoughtful questions to invite connection and reflection. (Luke 24:17 – "What are you discussing together as you walk along?")

Pro Tip: Don't force the moment. Just being there—with an open heart and closed mouth—is sometimes **the most powerful thing you can do.**

Even when they don't talk, your presence says: *"You matter. I'm here. And I'll still be here when you're ready."* 💛

So keep the engine running, **Player 1.** You never know when the next turn will lead to a deeper connection. 🚗✨

Side Quests!

As your teen steps further into independence, **side quests become powerful ways to stay connected without pressure or lectures.** These mini-missions create space for **shared interests, laughter, and trust-building**—on their terms.

📖 **Biblical Encouragement:** *"Rejoice with those who rejoice; mourn with those who mourn. Live in harmony with one another."* — Romans 12:15–16

🎧 PLAYLIST EXCHANGE QUEST

◆ **Objective:** Build connection through shared music.

◆ **How to Play:**

🎮 Create playlists for each other.

🎮 Include songs that make you think of them, or reflect your mood, memories, or values.

🎮 Listen together and talk about why you chose each track.

◆ **Reward:**

✓ Sparks meaningful conversation

✓ Shows mutual appreciation and curiosity

✓ Offers insight into your teen's world and emotions

📖 *"Sing to the Lord a new song; sing to the Lord, all the earth."* — Psalm 96:1

(*Translation: Music is a sacred tool for connection and expression.*)

⚒ PROJECT PARTNER CHALLENGE

◆ **Objective:** Join forces on something your teen is excited about.

◆ **How to Play:**

🎮 Ask them what they'd love help with:
- Redecorating their room
- Filming or editing a video
- Planning a family event or celebration

    🎮 Let them **take the lead** while you support and assist.

◆ **Reward:**

✓ Builds trust and teamwork

✓ Gives them ownership and confidence

✓ Creates shared memories that last

📖 *"Two are better than one... if either of them falls down, one can help the other up." — Ecclesiastes 4:9–10*

 Pro Tip: The more your teen feels seen, heard, and supported, the more likely they are to invite you into their world. These quests might look simple—but **they unlock deep, lasting connection.**

Now go forth, **Player 1.** Side quests may not be required, but they're where some of the most powerful growth—and joy—happens. 💛🚀

 # Troubleshooting Guide

Issue	Fix
My teen spends all their time on their phone.	Set clear screen-time boundaries and model healthy habits yourself. Create screen-free times, like during meals or before bed.
They shut down and won't talk to me.	Give them space but let them know you're available. Use low-pressure moments, like car rides, to start conversations.
They push back on every rule.	Involve them in setting boundaries and explain the reasoning behind rules. This gives them a sense of control and responsibility.
They seem overwhelmed by schoolwork and responsibilities.	Help them prioritise tasks by breaking them into manageable steps. Teach them time management skills, like using a planner or to-do list.
They're constantly comparing themselves to their peers.	Emphasise their unique strengths and accomplishments. Encourage them to focus on personal growth rather than competition.
They make impulsive or risky decisions.	Use mistakes as learning opportunities. Talk about consequences without judgment: "What do you think you could do differently next time?"
They struggle with self-esteem.	Validate their feelings and remind them of their value beyond achievements. Help them identify activities that build confidence and joy.
They resist family activities.	Let them help plan family time so they feel invested. Keep activities flexible and

	fun, like a movie night or cooking a meal together.

 Pro Tip for Troubleshooting

Teens are deep in the process of discovering **who they are, what they believe, and where they belong.** It's a time of growth, questioning, and occasional chaos—and they need you more than ever (even if they act like they don't).

Your role is evolving. You're no longer the **manager of their every move**, but the **mentor who walks beside them**.

✅ **Be present without hovering.**
✅ **Listen without judgment.**
✅ **Guide without controlling.**

📖 **Biblical Encouragement:** *"The purposes of a person's heart are deep waters, but one who has insight draws them out."* — *Proverbs 20:5*

Mentorship is your ultimate cheat code—because teens don't just need answers; they need someone who believes in them while they figure things out.

Stay steady, stay kind, and stay curious. You're helping them build the character, confidence, and courage they'll carry into adulthood. 💛✨

Final Boss Battle:

Surviving Parenthood and Keeping Your Sanity Intact

Welcome to the Final Boss Battle

After navigating countless levels, battling tantrums, threenager meltdowns, dramatic sighs, and epic snack negotiations, you've arrived at the **Final Boss Battle**:
Surviving Parenthood and Keeping Your Sanity Intact.
But here's the twist—**this level isn't about your child. It's about you.**
Your mission now? To **reflect on the journey**, celebrate your wins (even the messy ones), and keep growing right alongside your child. Because parenting doesn't really end—it just evolves.

📖 *"Let us not become weary in doing good, for at the proper time we will reap a harvest if we do not give up."* — *Galatians 6:9*

Core Mission: Care for the Caregiver

You've been the steady hand, the midnight nurse, the snack baron, the emotional anchor, and the boss battle strategist. Now it's time to turn some of that care back toward yourself.

🛠 **How to care for the caregiver:**
- **Prioritise your wellbeing**—your physical, emotional, and spiritual health matter.
- **Celebrate your wins,** not just your kid's.
- **Acknowledge the hard days** without shame—they're proof that you're in the game and giving it your all.
- **Let go of perfection.** Parenting is not a performance—it's a relationship.

📖 *"He restores my soul."* — *Psalm 23:3*

The Final Boss Battle: The Guilt Gremlin

The **Guilt Gremlin** is a sneaky, shape-shifting foe. It creeps in during quiet moments—especially when you're reflecting on your parenting journey. It whispers things like:
"Did I do enough?"
"What if I messed them up?"
"Other parents do it better."
It feeds on self-doubt and thrives in the shadows of comparison, trying to **overshadow your faithfulness with fear.**

📖 **Biblical Truth:** *"There is now no condemnation for those who are in Christ Jesus." — Romans 8:1*
You are not failing—you are learning, loving, and growing. That's the real win.

🛡 How to Defeat the Guilt Gremlin

◆ 1. Flip the Script

When the Gremlin says, *"You failed,"* respond with:
"I learned."

Mistakes are inevitable in parenting. What matters is how you **grow through them—not whether you avoid them.**

📖 *"His power is made perfect in weakness."* — *2 Corinthians 12:9*

◆ 2. Celebrate the Wins

Think about the times you showed up:
- The bedtime hugs after a hard day.
- The patience you found when you had none left.
- The times you said, "I'm sorry," and meant it.

Those moments matter. Every act of love is a victory.

◆ 3. Practice Self-Compassion

Talk to yourself like you would talk to your child.
Would you shame them for being human?
Or would you say, *"You're doing your best. I see you. I love you."*
Offer yourself the same grace.

📖 *"Love your neighbor as yourself."* — *Mark 12:31*
(Hint: That includes how you love yourself.)

 Pro Tip: Gratitude is the Gremlin's kryptonite. When doubts creep in, write down **three things you're proud of** as a parent. Big or small, they're proof that you're showing up—and that's more than enough.

You don't have to be perfect to be powerful.
You just have to keep playing with love. 💛

Gameplay Hazards

Just when you think you've made it through every parenting stage, **a few stealthy hazards sneak in under the radar**. These aren't about tantrums or bedtime battles—these ones target **you**, Player 1.

But don't worry—you've gained wisdom, courage, and a great set of cheat codes. Let's expose these end-level threats and take them down together.

📖 **Biblical Encouragement:** *"Let us throw off everything that hinders... and run with perseverance the race marked out for us." — Hebrews 12:1*

👀 The Comparison Monster

This sneaky villain whispers, *"Other parents are doing better than you."* It scrolls alongside you on social media and lurks at school drop-off, convincing you that you're falling behind.

🛠 **How to Beat It:**

🎮 Focus on your own family's journey.

🎮 Remind yourself: **No family is the same.** No story is identical.

🎮 Your **love, presence, and effort matter more than perfection.**

📖 *"Each one should test their own actions. Then they can take pride in themselves alone, without comparing themselves to someone else."* — Galatians 6:4

🧙 The "What-If" Wizard
This sneaky trickster **casts spells of regret and anxiety**, replaying the past and fast-forwarding worst-case scenarios about the future.

⚒️ How to Beat It:
🎮 Stay grounded in the **present moment**—this is where parenting happens.

🎮 Remind yourself: **God is already in the future, and He has grace for the past.**

📖 *"Do not worry about tomorrow, for tomorrow will worry about itself."* — Matthew 6:34

☐ The Empty Fuel Bar
You've given so much—time, energy, emotional support—that your own tank is running low. It's not failure. It's **fatigue**.

⚒️ How to Beat It:
🎮 Prioritize **regular self-care**—not as a luxury, but as survival.

🎮 Refill your soul with **rest, relationships, and even small moments of peace.**

🎮 Remember: **You matter, too.**

📖 *"Come with me by yourselves to a quiet place and get some rest."* — Mark 6:31

Pro Tip: These hazards don't make you weak—they prove you've been fighting hard for something that matters.

You've poured yourself out in love. Now it's time to **refuel with grace.** 💛

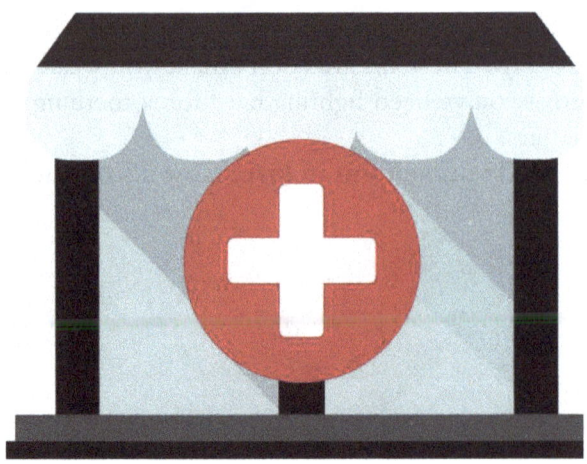

Cheat Codes

You've unlocked wisdom, resilience, and a few well-earned scars along the way. These **Final Level Cheat Codes** aren't just about getting through the day—they're about **finishing the level with purpose, presence, and peace.**

📖 **Biblical Encouragement:** *"The one who calls you is faithful, and he will do it."* — 1 Thessalonians 5:24

☐ The Reflection Buff
◆ Take a moment to **look back on the early levels**—the sleepless nights, the snack bandits, the dramatic threenager episodes.
◆ See how far your child has come… and **how far you've come, too.**
◆ You've grown in patience, wisdom, and love. **That's worth honouring.**

📖 *"Forget not all His benefits—who redeems your life from the pit and crowns you with love and compassion."* — Psalm 103:2–4

💎 The Connection Treasure

◆ Even as your child grows older and more independent, **one-on-one time still matters.**

◆ Prioritise connection—**a walk, a coffee date, a game night, a late-night chat.**

◆ These moments are the glue that **holds your relationship together in every season.**

📖 *"Where your treasure is, there your heart will be also."* — *Matthew 6:21*

✅ The "Good Enough" Hack

◆ Perfection is a myth.

◆ Let go of the pressure to be everything, fix everything, or always get it right.

◆ Your child doesn't need a perfect parent—**they need a present one.**

📖 *"My grace is sufficient for you, for my power is made perfect in weakness."* — *2 Corinthians 12:9*

Pro Tip:

These final cheat codes are about **perspective**—seeing that parenting isn't about completing the level flawlessly.

It's about **showing up, growing up, and loving deeply**, every step of the way.

You're not just surviving—you're shaping a legacy. 💛

Save Point: The Bigger Picture

Parenting is a series of **endless quests**—some thrilling, some exhausting, many requiring restarts. You've battled bosses, navigated side quests, and leveled up in patience, wisdom, and resilience.

But through it all, there are **Save Points**—tiny, powerful moments that remind you why you keep playing.

💛 A whispered *"thank you"* from the backseat.

💛 An unexpected hug in the middle of a tough day.

💛 A shared laugh during a kitchen disaster.

These aren't interruptions to the game. **They're the reward.**

Why Save Points Matter
These sacred moments may seem small, but they're the **real treasures**—the ones that fuel your heart and bring purpose to the chaos. They remind you that even in the mess and uncertainty, **something beautiful is being built**:
A relationship rooted in **love, trust, and connection.**

📖 *"Children are a heritage from the Lord, offspring a reward from him."* — *Psalm 127:3*

So when the level feels hard, when the screen goes fuzzy with doubt and fatigue—**pause.** Look around.

Find the Save Point.

 Pro Tip: Keep seeking and savouring those small but sacred moments.
They are **the real treasure of the game.**
They are **God's way of reminding you—you're doing holy work.** 🩶

You've played well, Player 1. And the adventure?
It's far from over. 🚀 ✨

.

 Troubleshooting Guide

Issue	Fix
I feel like I didn't do enough.	Remind yourself that parenting isn't about being perfect; it's about showing up. Reflect on moments you did your best—and celebrate them.
I miss the early stages.	Nostalgia is natural. Use those feelings to celebrate how far your child has come and find joy in their current stage.
Parenting feels like it's never-ending.	Shift your mindset: It's not about finishing—it's about enjoying the ride. Focus on the connection, not the completion.
I feel disconnected from my child now that they're older.	Find shared interests or create new traditions. Even small rituals, like a weekly coffee date or family movie night, can reignite connection.
I don't know what my role is now.	Your role has evolved into mentor and supporter. Offer guidance when asked, and respect their growing independence.

Pro Tip for Troubleshooting

Parenting is a **marathon, not a sprint.** It's messy, miraculous, exhausting, and holy—all at the same time.
You won't get everything right. No one does.
But **your mistakes don't define you—**
your willingness to learn, grow, and keep showing up does.
So **celebrate the small wins**—the deep breaths taken instead of yelling, the "I love you" whispered after a rough day, the peanut butter sandwich that doubled as dinner and comfort food.

📖 *"His mercies are new every morning." — Lamentations 3:23*

You don't have to be perfect.
Good enough is more than enough.
Because your child doesn't need a flawless parent—
They need you. 💛

Epilogue: The Journey Continues

There's no true *"Game Over"* in parenting. No credits rolling. No final score.

Instead, it's a **lifelong adventure**—a journey of **evolving roles, growing connection, and sacred, shared moments.**

Each level brought its own challenges and joys. The quests may change—school runs turn into uni drop-offs, snack negotiations into life advice—but the **bond you've built remains constant**.

You've navigated **God's parenting game** with **resilience, faith, love, and a healthy dose of humour.**

You've failed forward. You've grown.

You've shown up again and again—and **that's what matters most.**

📖 *"Being confident of this, that He who began a good work in you will carry it on to completion..."* — *Philippians 1:6*

So, Player 1—
Keep playing with purpose.
Keep learning as you go.
Keep loving deeply.
You're not just parenting.
You're leveling up—every single day.
And that's something to be proud of. 🎮 💛

Achievement Unlocked: Parenthood Complete (For Now).

Afterword: God's parenting game—Why Connection Matters

Parenting is the ultimate open-world game: there are no maps, no clear instructions, and certainly no pause button. Just when you think you've figured out one level, the game shifts, introducing new challenges, mini-bosses, and the occasional (or frequent) tantrum. And yet, it's the most immersive, life-changing adventure you'll ever undertake.

In *God's parenting game*, we wanted to capture the essence of this journey—not as a manual that promises perfection (because that's not real) but as a guide to help you navigate the ups, downs, and sideways twists with humour, heart, and a little more clarity. Why gaming as a theme? Because parenting is a lot like a video game: it's messy, unpredictable, and at times frustrating, but it's also joyful, rewarding, and full of "Save Point" moments that make it all worthwhile.

Why We Wrote This Book
Between the two of us, we've logged over 40 years in education and 16 years in the trenches of parenting. We've taught thousands of children, worked with their families, and parented our own kids through meltdowns, eye-rolls, and awkward school photos. What we've learned through these experiences is simple but profound: **connection is the foundation of everything.**

Whether you're navigating Level 1 with a newborn or bracing yourself for the Final Boss Battle with a teenager, the same principle holds true: your child's sense of security, resilience, and authenticity comes from knowing you're there for them. The way you show up—imperfectly but consistently—has a profound impact not just on their childhood but on who they'll become as adults.

But we also know this is easier said than done. Parenting is hard, messy, and often feels like stumbling through a dark cave with no torch. That's why we structured this book the way we did: to provide both practical tools and a light-hearted framework to help you navigate the adventure without losing your sanity (or your sense of humour).

The Two Core Themes: Attachment and Authenticity.

At its heart, *God's parenting game* is built around two interconnected themes: **attachment** and **authenticity.** These aren't just buzzwords; they're the guiding stars of effective, connected parenting.

1. **Attachment:**
    - In the early levels of parenting, attachment is everything. When your baby cries, they're asking one fundamental question: "Is someone here for me?" Your response teaches them that the world is safe and that they can trust others.
    - This isn't about being perfect. Attachment is built through small, everyday moments: locking eyes during a feeding, rocking them to sleep, or responding to their cries with a calming touch. These acts, repeated consistently (not flawlessly), wire your child's brain for security and resilience.

2. **Authenticity:**
    - As your child grows, the balance begins to shift. The toddler who once clung to your leg now insists on pouring their own cereal. The school-age child starts defining themselves outside the family. The teenager challenges your rules, beliefs, and patience.
    - These are good things. Your child's authenticity—their ability to know and express who they truly are—depends on your willingness to let go, step back, and support their independence.

The trick is balancing these themes. Attachment and authenticity aren't opposites; they're complementary. A securely attached child feels safe enough to explore the world and be themselves, knowing that no matter what, you'll always be their anchor.

Why Humour Matters.

Let's be real: parenting can be absurd. One minute you're trying to have a deep conversation with your teenager about respect, and the next, you're stepping on a rogue LEGO in your bare feet. One moment your toddler is giggling uncontrollably, and the next, they're on the floor screaming because their banana broke in half. Humour isn't just a coping mechanism—it's a parenting superpower. It diffuses tension, strengthens connection, and reminds us not to take ourselves too seriously. That's why this book doesn't shy away from the ridiculousness of parenting. We believe that laughing at the chaos doesn't diminish its importance—it makes it more bearable.

The Importance of Play.

We've seen it time and time again in classrooms, at home, and in our own lives: **play is where connection happens.** That's why we included side quests in every level. These aren't just cute activities to kill time—they're intentional opportunities to bond, spark joy, and create memories.
- In Level 1, tummy time isn't just about strengthening muscles; it's about cheering on your baby as they learn to lift their head, showing them that you're their biggest fan.
- In Level 4, a DIY game night isn't just a way to avoid screen time; it's a chance to collaborate, laugh, and remind your child that family time is fun.
- Play evolves as your child grows, but its purpose remains the same: to build connection and trust in ways words alone can't.

Mistakes Are Part of the Game.

If there's one thing we want you to take away from this book, it's this: **you don't have to get it right every time.** Parenting isn't about perfection—it's about showing up, learning as you go, and repairing when you miss the mark.

The truth is, you will make mistakes. You'll lose your patience, say the wrong thing, or feel like you're failing. And that's okay. Mistakes are inevitable, but repair is powerful. Apologising, reconnecting, and trying again teaches your child that relationships are resilient—and so are you.

Why the Gaming Metaphor?

We didn't choose the gaming metaphor just because it's fun (though it is). We chose it because it reflects the reality of parenting:

- **Levels:** Each stage of your child's development brings new challenges and opportunities.
- **Big Bosses and Mini-Bosses:** From sleep deprivation to teenage rebellion, the obstacles are real, but they're also surmountable.
- **Cheat Codes:** Every parent needs a few life hacks to make the game easier.
- **Save Points:** These are the moments of connection, laughter, and pride that keep you going when the game gets tough.

Parenting isn't linear, and it doesn't have a "win state." It's a lifelong adventure, full of respawns, retries, and rewards. The gaming framework is our way of making this journey feel less daunting and more like what it is: an epic quest.

The Big Picture.

At its core, parenting is about building a relationship. It's not about raising a "perfect" child or being a "perfect" parent—it's about creating a bond that can weather tantrums, mistakes, and hard conversations. It's about showing your child, over and over, that they are loved, valued, and seen.

As educators and parents, we've witnessed the transformative power of connection. We've seen the child who struggles with schoolwork but thrives under a teacher who believes in them.

We've seen the teenager who tests every boundary but softens when their parent says, "I'm here if you need me." And we've felt it in our own lives—in the messy, magical, imperfect moments that make parenting so challenging and so worth it.

And through every level, every respawn, and every win, remember: you're not just playing the game—you're changing lives. One save point at a time.

"Above all, put on love, which binds everything together in perfect unity." — Colossians 3:14

The New 3Rs: Role-Modelling, Resilience, and *Not* Rescuing.

You've completed every level, faced every boss, and now you've unlocked a bonus expansion: the new 3Rs. These are the legacy-building skills—the ones that shape who your child becomes long after the game's early levels are complete.

Parenting today feels like navigating a tightrope. On one side is the instinct to protect—to smooth every bump, soothe every hurt, and solve every problem. On the other side is the need to foster independence—to equip our children to walk their own paths, face their own challenges, and build resilience. The balance is delicate, but crucial. In this chapter, we'll explore the new 3Rs of parenting: Role-Modelling, Resilience, and Not Rescuing. Together, these principles can help us raise capable, compassionate, and confident children in a world that often feels overwhelming.

Role-Modelling: They Learn What We Live

"Follow my example, as I follow the example of Christ." — 1 Corinthians 11:1

Our children are always watching. More than our words, it's our actions that shape their understanding of how to move through the world. If we tell them to be present, but are constantly checking our phones, the lesson they learn is that distraction is acceptable. If we encourage them to be curious but respond to their endless questions with sighs of frustration, they learn that curiosity is a burden.

Role-modelling means living the behaviours we want to instil. It's about demonstrating patience when the queue at the supermarket crawls, empathy when a neighbour is struggling, and curiosity when we stop to marvel at a starry night sky. It also means modelling vulnerability—sharing stories of our own childhood struggles, the mistakes we made, and how we learned from them.

For instance, if your child is anxious about presenting at school, resist the urge to dismiss their fear with "You'll be fine." Instead, share your own experience: "I remember feeling nervous before work presentations. I even felt my heart race. Here's what helped me: I took a deep breath, focused on one friendly face, and reminded myself I'd prepared well." In that moment, you've role-modelled vulnerability, emotional regulation, and problem-solving.

Psychologist Albert Bandura's social learning theory highlights that children learn behaviours through observation, imitation, and modelling. When they see us manage stress calmly, engage with curiosity, and practice kindness, they are more likely to replicate those behaviours.

Another practical example: if you want your child to develop healthy digital habits, start by examining your own. Are you scrolling through your phone during conversations? Try setting up family-wide screen-free times, like during dinner or before bed. When children witness parents setting boundaries with technology, they're more likely to follow suit.

Resilience: Built Through Safe, Supported Struggles

"Not only so, but we also glory in our sufferings, because we know that suffering produces perseverance." — Romans 5:3

Resilience isn't something a child magically develops in isolation. It grows when children face challenges with the scaffolding of a safe, supportive adult beside them. Too often, resilience is misunderstood as toughness or independence. In reality, resilience is the ability to bounce back because a child knows they have a secure foundation to fall back on.

When a toddler falls while learning to walk, we instinctively smile and say, "Oops! Up you get!" We don't berate them for falling or rush to carry them everywhere. The same principle applies as they grow older. When they forget their lunchbox, resist the urge to drop it off at school. Instead, use it as an opportunity to brainstorm strategies together: "What could help you remember tomorrow? Maybe we could put a sticky note on the front door or set an alarm."

The discomfort of natural consequences, paired with compassionate guidance, becomes the training ground for resilience. They learn I can handle challenges. I can solve problems. I am supported, but capable.

Dr. Gabor Maté emphasizes the importance of co-regulation: children borrow our calm when they are distressed. A study published in Developmental Psychology found that children who had parents who coached them through emotional challenges were better able to manage stress later in life. This highlights that resilience is not a solo Endeavor—it is co-created through relationship.

Practical examples can make this abstract concept clearer. Imagine a child struggling with a difficult homework assignment. The instinct might be to sit down and help solve each problem. A more resilience-building approach is to sit nearby and say, "This looks challenging. What's your plan to tackle it? Want to brainstorm some strategies together?" The child learns problem-solving without feeling abandoned.

Not Rescuing: Guiding, Not Fixing

"Each one should carry their own load." — Galatians 6:5

The desire to rescue our children from discomfort is deeply human. No parent wants to see their child hurt, frustrated, or anxious. Yet, when we habitually step in to fix things, we inadvertently send the message: "You can't handle this." Over time, children either become dependent on us to solve their problems or internalize a belief that the world is too overwhelming for them.

Not rescuing doesn't mean abandoning. It means sitting beside them in their discomfort, offering empathy, and guiding them toward solutions. Picture a child struggling with a friendship issue. The rescuing response might be to call the other child's parent or suggest they find new friends. The non-rescuing response is to sit alongside, listen, and ask: "What do you think might help here? Want to brainstorm some ideas together?"

In adolescence, this principle becomes even more critical. If your teenager wants a part-time job, don't phone businesses on their behalf. Instead, help them create a resume, role-play interview scenarios, and talk through potential challenges. When they land the job, the pride they feel will be rooted in their effort—not in your intervention.

We can't understate the importance of connection in overcoming life's difficulties. By supporting children to face challenges side-by-side, rather than removing obstacles for them, we foster both their resilience and their trust in us as dependable guides.

The Power of Affirmation and Avoiding Shame

Throughout this process, our language matters. Children learn best in an environment where mistakes are seen as part of growth, not as failures to be ashamed of. Avoiding shame doesn't mean avoiding accountability. It means framing mistakes as learning opportunities.

Instead of, "Why can't you remember your bag?" try, "Packing your bag can be tricky—what might help you remember tomorrow?"

Affirm their feelings, even when those feelings are hard to witness. If they say, "I hate school," resist the urge to correct or dismiss. Instead, respond with curiosity: "That sounds tough.

What's been hard about it lately?" This approach builds trust, teaches emotional intelligence, and communicates that all emotions are normal and manageable.

Andrew Lines, who developed the Rites of Passage Framework, emphasizes the importance of helping children navigate life's challenges while affirming their inherent worth. When parents respond to distress with empathy rather than dismissal, children learn that all emotions are valid and manageable.

Our Own Baggage: Parenting from Self-Awareness

Finally, parenting with the new 3Rs requires self-awareness. Our own childhood experiences shape how we respond to our children's struggles. If we were raised to "just get on with it," we might dismiss our child's emotions. If we were excessively protected, we might overcorrect by pushing independence too soon.

Take time to reflect: How did your parents handle discomfort? What messages did you internalize about mistakes, emotions, and challenges? When we parent from a place of awareness rather than reaction, we can consciously choose responses that align with our long-term goals for our children.

Mel Robbins often speaks about the power of modelling self-awareness. If we notice ourselves reacting harshly, we can pause, name the feeling, and later share with our child: "I was really stressed earlier and snapped. I'm sorry about that. I'm working on taking deep breaths when I feel overwhelmed." In doing so, we model both accountability and emotional regulation.

Conclusion: Walking Beside, Not Carrying

The new 3Rs—Role-Modelling, Resilience, and Not Rescuing—are not about perfection. We will all have moments of impatience, worry, or intervention. The goal is to shift our default from fixing to guiding, from telling to showing, from rescuing to reassuring.

When we walk beside our children instead of carrying them, we give them the greatest gift: the belief that they can navigate life's challenges with courage, creativity, and confidence—because they've seen it modelled, practiced it with support, and experienced the pride of overcoming difficulties on their own.

This isn't a side quest—it's the legacy stage. When you guide with grace, model with honesty, and step back with trust, you're not just raising a child. You're equipping a future adult—resilient, authentic, and deeply connected to the love that shaped them.

For those with more time! (Informative and inspirational reads)

Bandura, A. (1977). Social Learning Theory. Prentice Hall.

Maté, G. (2008). In the Realm of Hungry Ghosts: Close Encounters with Addiction. Knopf Canada.

Hari, J. (2018). Lost Connections: Uncovering the Real Causes of Depression – and the Unexpected Solutions. Bloomsbury Publishing.

Lines, A. The Rites of Passage Framework (various publications).

Robbins, M. (2017). The 5 Second Rule: Transform your Life, Work, and Confidence with Everyday Courage. Savio Republic.

A Final Word.

If you've made it this far—**thank you**.
Thank you for showing up, for seeking wisdom, for leaning into the mess and magic of parenting. Whether you're holding a newborn, navigating toddler chaos, or facing off with a teen-level boss battle, we want you to know this:

👉 **You're doing better than you think.**

Parenting is the **hardest, holiest game you'll ever play**. It's complex, unpredictable, and filled with challenges you didn't see coming.
But it's also **beautiful**—full of wonder, deep love, unexpected laughter, and sacred Save Points that remind you: *This matters.*
There's no pause button. But there is grace.
There are second chances.
And there is a God who walks with you, even in the loading screens.
So keep showing up.
Keep finding joy in the little wins.
Keep playing—with heart, with humour, and with hope.

📖 *"Let us run with perseverance the race marked out for us..."* — *Hebrews 12:1*

Achievement Unlocked: You're an incredible parent.

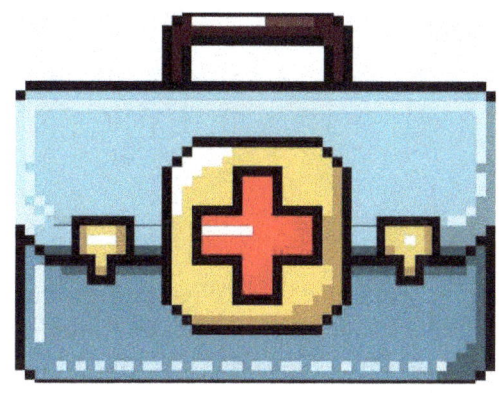

Tear out in case of emergency!

HELP...

... Surviving a Level 10 Meltdown (Yours)

Parenting Rage Quit: Navigating Anger and Frustration Without Losing a Life

Let's be honest: sometimes God's parenting game is set to the hardest difficulty level—no map, no instructions, and a constant barrage of side quests like "Find the Lost Shoe" and "Why is the Milk in the Pantry?" Anger and frustration are part of the package. If you've picked up this book mid-rage, welcome. You're exactly where you need to be.

Step 1: Press Pause

First, stop. Breathe. You don't have to solve this right now. Anger makes us reactive, not reflective. It's like when your kid does something ridiculous, and you're standing there thinking, 'Why...why are you like this?' And then you remember: oh yeah, they share my DNA.

Quick Pause Tricks:

The 5-5-5 Breath: Inhale for 5 seconds, hold for 5, exhale for 5. Repeat until your inner voice says, "Aye, calm doon."

The Angry Cup of Tea: Announce, "I'm making a cup of tea to save us both." Bonus: your child learns that emotions can be managed, not unleashed.

The Exit Stage Left: If safe, step outside for a moment. There's no problem so big that you can't walk away from it for a minute...except maybe stepping on Lego.

Step 2: Decode the Rage Monster

Anger is often a surface emotion, with worry, exhaustion, or unmet expectations lurking underneath. Anger protects our boundaries. But when we parent from it, we lose connection.

Ask Yourself:

What boundary was crossed? (Respect, safety, sanity?)

What do I actually need here? (Quiet, cooperation, fewer existential questions at bedtime?)

What's going on with my child? (Are they tired, overwhelmed, or testing limits?)

And here's a gem: sometimes we're angry because kids are just...kids. Like when your three-year-old insists on putting shoes on the dog because "he wants to go to the park." He doesn't. He wants his dignity back.

Step 3: Deploy the Humour Hack

Humour diffuses tension like nothing else. Laughter doesn't just lighten the mood—it gives you a mental reset and reminds everyone that you're a team, not opponents.

Tactical Humour Moves:

The Silly Reset: Do an over-the-top fake meltdown: "Oh no! The dishwasher's not unloaded! The world will end!" Guaranteed eye-rolls but also laughter.

The Accent Challenge: Deliver your next instruction in a ridiculous accent. Try "Brush your teeth" with a pirate growl.

The Shared Joke: "I need a break before I turn into Grumpy McParentface."

Someone has always had it worse!
My friend once spent an entire evening looking for her son's school library book called The Sneaky Squirrel. She tore the house apart. Next morning, her son casually announced, "Oh yeah, I buried it in the garden so the squirrel could find its family."

Laughter doesn't erase the frustration, but it shrinks it down to a manageable size.

Step 4: Repair, Don't Ruminate

We all lose it sometimes. What matters is what comes next.

The Parenting Repair Script:

"I was really frustrated earlier and I yelled. I'm sorry for that. Let's figure out how to solve this together."

"Everyone gets angry—it's a normal feeling. The trick is learning what to do with it. Want to brainstorm our own Anger Playbook?"

"I love you, even when I'm mad. Always."

Someone has always had it worse!
A dad I know tried to apologise for yelling at his son. The kid said, "It's okay, Dad. I've heard worse on YouTube." Cue a family meeting on internet safety.

Step 5: Build an Anger Game Plan

Think of this as a cheat code for next time.

Anger Playbook Checklist:

Trigger ID: What situations push your buttons? (Homework refusal, bedtime debates, "Can I have a snack?" three seconds after dinner.)

Pause Plan: What will you do when anger flares? (Breath, tea, a quick "walk-off" like a footballer protesting a red card.)

Communicate Calm: How will you explain your feelings to your child without blame? ("I need a minute to cool down because I want to talk calmly with you.")

Practice Together: Help your child create their own anger plan. Show them that emotional self-regulation is a skill, not magic.

Someone has always had it worse!
A mum told me her teenager was always forgetting lunch. One day she said, "Fine, you'll figure it out." The kid did—by ordering a triple cheeseburger, fries, and a smoothie delivered to school. Lesson learned: resilience isn't always nutritious.

Parenting Is a Contact Sport (Emotionally, at Least)

Anger isn't failure. It's a sign that you care. You're not alone—every parent has their "I'm gonna lose it" moments. There's no such thing as bad weather, just bad clothes. In parenting terms: there's no such thing as a bad parent, just a parent learning new emotional gear.

"The Lord is gracious and compassionate, slow to anger and rich in love." – Psalm 145:8

So go on—breathe, laugh, and know that turning this page instead of turning into the Hulk? That's already a parenting win.

Resources:

Survival Pack

Parent Power-Ups: Quick Recharge Strategies for Every Schedule

This section offers **10-minute**, **30-minute**, and **1-hour** self-care ideas for busy parents. Think of them as "power-ups" to keep you feeling balanced and recharged during God's parenting game.

10-Minute Power-Ups

- ☐ **The Breathing Boost:** Close your eyes, inhale deeply for 4 seconds, hold for 4, exhale for 4, and repeat for 5 cycles.
- ☐ **Coffee or Tea Time-Out:** Sip your favourite drink—slowly, without multitasking.
- ☐ **Gratitude Snapshot:** Write down 3 things you're grateful for today, even if they're small wins.
- ☐ **Micro-Meditation:** Use a meditation app or a calming playlist for a quick mental reset.
- ☐ **Sunshine Sprint:** Step outside for fresh air and a quick walk around the block.
- ☐ **Stretch to Reset:** Do 5 stretches focusing on your back, shoulders, and neck.
- ☐ **Laugh Break:** Watch a short, funny video or read a few pages from a humorous book.
- ☐ **Mini-Journal:** Write down one thought or feeling to process and release it.
- ☐ **Dance Break:** Put on an energising song and move like nobody's watching.
- ☐ **Skin Reset:** Apply a face mask or simply splash cold water on your face for an instant refresh.

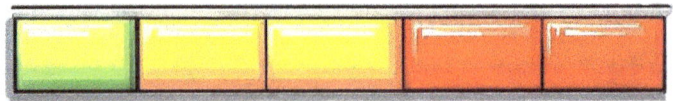

30-Minute Power-Ups

- ☐ **Yoga Flow:** Follow a 20–30 minute yoga video focusing on relaxation or energy.
- ☐ **Unplug and Read:** Pick up a book or magazine you love—bonus points if it's unrelated to parenting!
- ☐ **Nature Recharge:** Take a leisurely walk in a park or sit in your backyard with a cup of tea.
- ☐ **Call a Friend:** Connect with someone who makes you feel supported or inspired.
- ☐ **Creative Escape:** Draw, write, bake, or engage in a hobby that brings you joy.
- ☐ **Bubble Bath Bliss:** Light a candle, put on calming music, and soak away the stress.
- ☐ **Meal Prep Zen:** Prepare a simple, nourishing meal or snack just for yourself.
- ☐ **Declutter One Space:** Tidy a small area, like a drawer or your desk, for a mental refresh.
- ☐ **Guided Meditation or Mindfulness Session:** Use an app or YouTube to dive deeper into relaxation.
- ☐ **Exercise Burst:** Do a home workout or brisk walk to get your heart pumping.

1-Hour Power-Ups

- ☐ **Spa at Home:** Take a long bath, exfoliate, moisturise, and indulge in a mini spa treatment.
- ☐ **Go Solo:** Visit a café or bookstore alone for uninterrupted "me" time.
- ☐ **Mindful Meal:** Cook and savour a meal at your own pace, with zero interruptions.
- ☐ **Movie Escape:** Watch a feel-good movie or TV episode—guilt-free!
- ☐ **Date with a Hobby:** Paint, knit, garden, play music, or dive into something that's purely yours.
- ☐ **Power Nap:** Give yourself permission to nap and recharge fully.
- ☐ **Nature Immersion:** Go for a hike or a longer stroll in a calming natural setting.
- ☐ **Podcast and Chill:** Listen to an inspiring or entertaining podcast while relaxing.
- ☐ **Deep Declutter:** Organize a space that's been bothering you—like your closet or pantry.
- ☐ **Workout or Class:** Attend a fitness class, swim, or dedicate an hour to your favourite exercise.

 # QR Code References

Listen   *Watch*

Level 1

Podcast:
"The Birth Hour"
This podcast shares birth stories and experiences, offering support and insights for new parents navigating the early months.
Thriving Mum

YouTube Video:
"Dr Karp 5 S"
Swaddle, Side position, Shush, Swing, Suck (a pacifier or feed).
Dr Karp 5 s's

"The Single Most Important Parenting Strategy"
Clinical psychologist Dr. Becky Kennedy discusses effective parenting strategies.
YouTube

Level 2

Podcast:
"Respectful Parenting: Janet Lansbury Unruffled"
Janet Lansbury addresses common toddler behaviours and offers respectful parenting advice.
Mighty Kids Academy

YouTube Video:
"Master Positive Parenting: 10 Expert Tips"
This video provides practical tips for positive parenting during the toddler years.
YouTube

Level 3

Podcast:
"But Why: A Podcast for Curious Kids"
This podcast answers questions from curious kids, making it perfect for preschoolers and their parents.
Parents

YouTube Video:
"Your Child's Behaviour | 5 to 6 Years | Good Parenting Videos"
This video offers insights into managing behaviours typical of preschool-aged children.
YouTube

Level 4

Podcast:
"Mom and Dad Are Fighting"
Hosted by Slate, this podcast provides advice for parenting school-aged children.
Parents

YouTube Video:
"Listening to the Heart of Your Kids"
This video emphasises the importance of listening to your children during the school years.
YouTube

Listen

Watch

Level 5

Podcast:
"Good Inside with Dr. Becky"
Clinical psychologist Dr. Becky Kennedy offers parenting advice relevant to the tween years.
Parents

YouTube Video:
"5 Expert Tips No Parent Should Miss | Positive Parenting"
This video compiles expert advice beneficial for parents of tweens.
YouTube

Level 6

Podcast:
"Talking to Teens: Expert Tips for Parenting Teenagers"
This podcast offers insights and advice for parents navigating the teenage years.
Parents

YouTube Video:
"The Single Most Important Parenting Strategy"
Dr. Becky Kennedy discusses strategies that are also applicable to parenting teenagers.
YouTube

Listen

Watch

Notes & Scribbles

This space is yours. Use it to jot down insights, ideas, or just vent about the madness of parenting. Write down the brilliant parenting hack you invented at 2 a.m. Or the hilarious moment when your child announced, "Mum, I think the dog needs therapy."

Parenting isn't about perfection; it's about presence. And sometimes presence requires a bit of scribbling space.

(Feel free to doodle too. Stick-figure family portraits encouraged.)

Kids Say the Funniest Things: A Space to Capture the Moments We Swear We'll Remember

Children have a magical ability to say the most hilarious, profound, and downright bizarre things—usually when we least expect it. We always promise ourselves we'll remember, but life moves on, and those little gems get lost.

Here's your spot. Scribble down the quirky quotes, the unexpected wisdom, and the laugh-out-loud moments. Whether it's the time they confidently declared, "I don't need a bedtime—I'm basically nocturnal now" or asked, "Why don't penguins wear socks?", these are the stories you'll want to revisit when they're taller, older, and definitely less interested in bedtime cuddles.

(Bonus tip: Read these back to your kids when they're teenagers. Embarrassment guaranteed.)

Parenting Wins Log

Space to record moments when they nailed it.

www.ingramcontent.com/pod-product-compliance
Lightning Source LLC
Chambersburg PA
CBHW060837190426
43197CB00040B/2665